Popular Mechanics

Miter Saw Fundamentals

Rick Peters

Hearst Books
A Division of Sterling Publishing Co., Inc.
New York

Production Staff

Design: Triad Design Group

Cover Design: Celia Fuller

Photography: Christopher J. Vendetta

Cover photos: Christopher J. Vendetta

Illustrations: Bob Crimi

Copy Editor: Barbara McIntosh Webb

Page Layout: Sandy Freeman

Index: Nan Badgett

Library of Congress Cataloging-in-Publication Data
Peters, Rick.
   Popular Mechanics workshop. Miter saw fundamentals : the complete guide / Rick Peters.
      p. cm.
   Includes index.
   ISBN-13: 978-1-58816-557-2
   ISBN-10: 1-58816-557-4
   1. Radial saws. 2. Woodwork. I. Title.
   TT186.P4625 2006
   684'.083--dc22

                                          2005037803

10 9 8 7 6 5 4 3 2 1

Published by Hearst Books
A Division of Sterling Publishing Co., Inc.
387 Park Avenue South, New York, NY 10016

Popular Mechanics and Hearst Books are trademarks of Hearst Communications, Inc.

www.popularmechanics.com

For information about custom editions, special sales, premium and corporate purchases, please contact Sterling Special Sales Department at 800-805-5489 or specialsales@sterlingpub.com.

Distributed in Canada by Sterling Publishing
c/o Canadian Manda Group, 165 Dufferin Street
Toronto, Ontario, Canada M6K 3H6

Distributed in Australia by Capricorn Link (Australia) Pty. Ltd.
P.O. Box 704, Windsor, NSW 2756 Australia

Manufactured in China

Sterling ISBN-13: 978-1-58816-557-2
       ISBN-10: 1-58816-557-4

Contents

ACKNOWLEDGMENTS

For all their help, advice, and support, I offer thanks to:

Jason Feldner of Bosch Power Tools and Accessories, for technical assistance and for supplying the superbly engineered miter saws and accessories used throughout this book.

Sara Ruth of Weber Shandwick for Delta Machinery, for providing a hardworking Delta miter saw and technical assistance.

Abby Bradford of Hitachi Power Tools, for supplying three of their well-made miter saws and technical information.

Jim Brewer of Freud Tools, for technical assistance and for supplying the super-high-quality miter saw blades used throughout this book.

Brad Witt of Woodhaven, for providing technical assistance as well as their contractor's fence that expands the cutting capabilities of any miter saw.

Heinz Mulertt of Bench Dog, for supplying their easy-to-use crown molding jig.

Fred Gunzner of Avenger Products for that company's add-on laser guide systems that let anyone cut faster and more accurately with any miter saw.

Christopher Vendetta, for taking great photographs under less-than-desirable conditions and under tight deadlines.

Sandy Freeman, consummate designer, whose creative talents are evident on every page of this book.

Bob Crimi, for superb technical illustrations.

Barb Webb, copyediting whiz, for ferreting out mistakes and gently suggesting corrections.

Heartfelt thanks to my constant inspiration: Cheryl, Lynne, Will, and Beth.

INTRODUCTION

It's hard to imagine working wood in a shop or at a jobsite without a power miter saw. But the fact is that these now ubiquitous saws didn't exist prior to 1960. The original compound miter saw (or chop saw, as it was referred to) that was introduced by Rockwell filled such a void in the market that this single tool quickly outsold all of their other tools.

Prior to the miter saw, woodworkers used a radial arm saw or a table saw to cut boards into manageable lengths; carpenters used portable circular saws; and trim carpenters relied on a miter box and a handsaw. Not only did the chop saw replace all these, but it also completed every task faster and with more accuracy. Add to this that the chop saw was portable and didn't cost a whole lot, and it's no wonder it became so popular.

What's also amazing is that 40 years later, many of today's miter saws are surprisingly similar to the original. Sure, manufacturers have increased the saw's cutting capacities and added bells and whistles, but the chopping motion still gets the job done. Besides increasing the size of the lumber that modern saws can handle, newer saws can handle angled and beveled cuts with great precision. Saw makers have even started adding laser guides on many saws so that you can line up cuts faster and more accurately.

Although mainly used as a crosscutting machine, a properly tuned and maintained miter saw can handle a wide variety of tasks. Modern miter saws can tackle the complex compound cuts required for installing crown molding, make repeat cuts for installing wainscoting, miter window and door casing with ease, and even cut dadoes for joinery.

In this book, we'll help you identify which miter saws and accessories are best for you. We'll cover basic and advanced techniques and show you how to make jigs and fixtures to expand the capabilities of your saw. Maintenance and repair is laid out in detail so you can keep your saw running in tip-top shape. And the final chapter details several projects that you can build with a miter saw.

—James Meigs

Editor-in-Chief, **Popular Mechanics**

HITACHI
C 12LCH
DIGITAL & LASER

LASER

HITACHI
C 10FCH
LASER

LASER

15   0   15   30

Choosing a Miter Saw

When miter saws first hit the consumer market in the early 1960s, we thought they'd be great for carpenters and trim carpenters—and they were. But we didn't really think of them as fine woodworking tools until manufacturers started adding more and more features to the saws. And along with the increased features came increased accuracy. When sliding compound miter saws were introduced, we were hooked and we haven't looked back. These versatile saws with ever-increasing capacities have all but replaced the radial arm saw in most woodworking shops. Miter saws are smaller, lighter, and more portable than the hefty and bulky stationary radial arm saws. Add to this the fact that they're more accurate and safer to use, and it's no wonder miter saws can be found in workshops around the world. In this chapter, we'll walk you through the various types of miter saws, show you what they're capable of, and then help you choose the one that's best for you.

Miter saws come in a wide array of shapes, sizes, and capacities. Types include chop saws, compound miter saws, and sliding compound miter saws. The two most common sizes (shown here) are 10" and 12".

Chop Saws

Although it may seem like miter saws have been around forever, they didn't exist until 1964, when Ed Niehaus, a tool designer for Rockwell, was asked to automate the tedious task of hand-sawing framing lumber and trim to size using a hand saw and a miter box. In particular, he set out to design a tool that could easily cut a 2×4 or piece of standard crown molding to length—accurately. Original design notes showed a saw that cut from overhead that moved up and down on tracks. But Ed realized that this would not be very stable, so he came up with a pivoting action. He then added a spring to return the saw to the upright position, a retractable blade guard, and even a dust port and a brake.

After three years of development, Rockwell introduced the model 34-010 power miter saw. The saw turned out to be so popular that it quickly outsold all other Rockwell tools. But Rockwell never patented the

design and so competing tool companies quickly launched their own versions—and the tool industry has never been the same. The original power miter saw, also called a chop saw—it got its nickname from its action—chops boards into smaller pieces across their width. Most of these saws are capable of making miter cuts where the saw carriage is rotated to an angle between 0 and 45 degrees, usually in both directions (bottom photo). These saws have limited use but are great for crosscutting boards to length. It's important to understand that the blade of the saw does not tilt—that's the next step of the evolutionary chain of the miter saw.

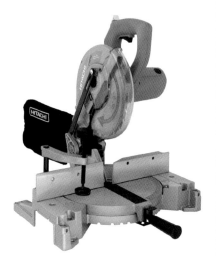

CHOP SAW ANATOMY

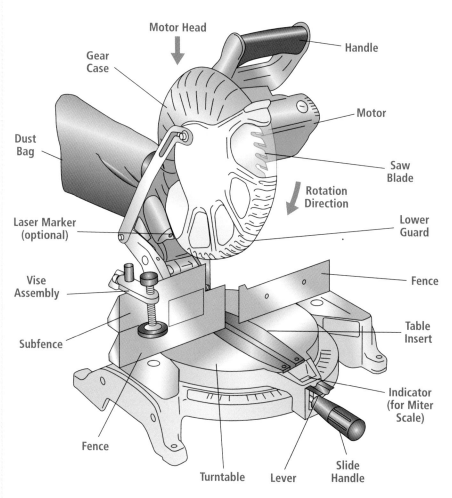

Compound Miter Saws

The next step in the evolution of the miter saw was the ability of the blade to tilt—originally only in one direction (from 0 to 45 degrees), but versions are now available that tilt in both directions. Couple this with the ability to pivot the blade, and you can cut compound miters with ease. This simple development eliminated complex jigs needed to hold and cut crown molding and other decorative trim.

Whether it's a chop saw, compound saw, or sliding compound saw (see page 10), all miter saws have common parts. They all basically consist of a table with a fence and a saw assembly that pivots up and down to make the cut. The saw assembly is made up of the motor, the blade and guard, and the handle and trigger. Depending on the type of saw, there may or may not be locking knobs that let you tilt the blade. All models have a knob or handle out front that's used to pivot the saw table for miter cuts. On better-quality saws, the table has a pair of adjustable plastic inserts near the kerf that you can move in or out to match the thickness of the blade. These basically serve as backer boards to help prevent splintering during the cut.

COMPOUND MITER SAW ANATOMY

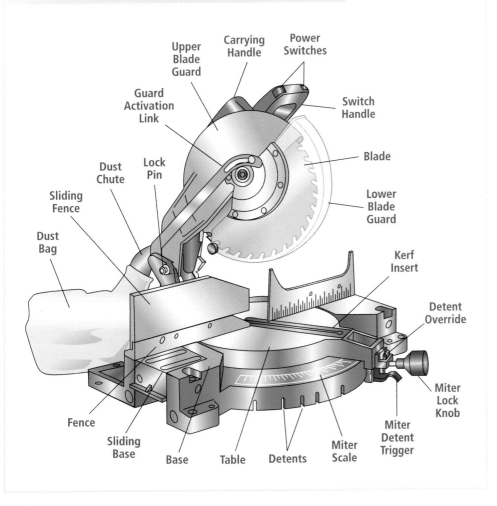

Sliding Compound Miter Saws

A sliding compound saw offers all the features of the compound saw, but has a saw carriage that slides, allowing you to cut wider boards. This type of saw has all but replaced the radial arm saw in most woodworking shops—and for good reason: Most have crosscut capacities of at least 12", they're extremely accurate, and they're portable. What more could you ask for?

It's easy to identify a sliding compound saw because of its track. The track may be on top (as shown here) or at the bottom (common to many Makita miter saws). The track may be a single post or dual posts like the Bosch saw shown here.

As with compound miter saws, when sliding miter saws were first introduced, they could tilt only in one direction. But newer versions allow you to tilt the blade to both the right and the left (typically 0 to 45 degrees or more) to make cutting molding easy. With a saw that only tilts in one direction, a certain amount of mental gymnastics is required to make a cut: You have to mentally flip the workpiece and the cutting angles. More than one piece of molding has been miscut because of this. Dual tilt eliminates this confusing practice.

SLIDING COMPOUND MITER SAW ANATOMY

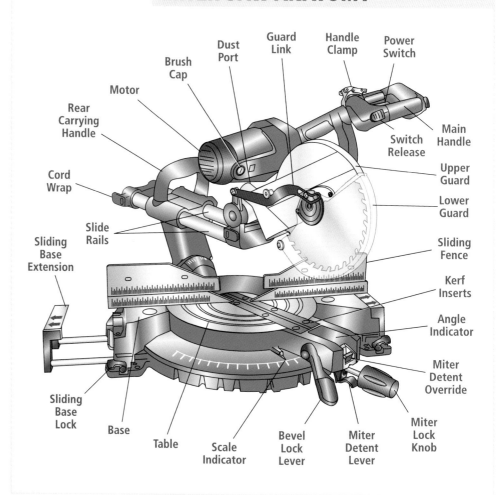

Brush Cap · Motor · Rear Carrying Handle · Dust Port · Guard Link · Handle Clamp · Power Switch · Switch Release · Main Handle · Upper Guard · Lower Guard · Cord Wrap · Slide Rails · Sliding Base Extension · Sliding Fence · Kerf Inserts · Angle Indicator · Miter Detent Override · Miter Lock Knob · Sliding Base Lock · Base · Table · Scale Indicator · Bevel Lock Lever · Miter Detent Lever · Miter Lock Knob

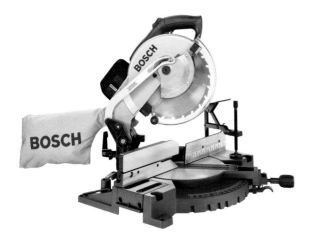

Cordless Miter Saws

Just when you thought they couldn't make a miter saw any better, they did. What could be better than a power miter saw? How about a power miter saw without a cord? That's exactly what Bosch Tools unveiled when they introduced the world's first 10" compound miter saw, as shown in the top photo and illustrated in the drawing below.

This saw sports a hefty 24-volt battery that can power through standard framing lumber and trim with ease. As with Bosch's other miter saws, it features an electric brake that will stop the blade in seconds, sliding fences for precise and accurate miter angles, and an easy-to-use and accurate detent system (including a useful detent override).

The Bosch 3924 truly makes a miter saw portable. Just imagine taking the saw wherever you need it without the hassle of dealing with a power cord.

CORDLESS MITER SAW ANATOMY

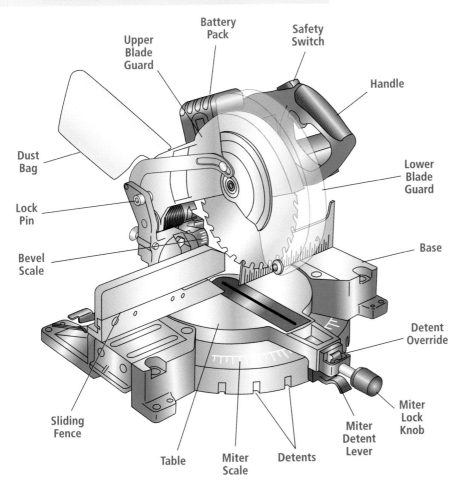

Upper Blade Guard
Battery Pack
Safety Switch
Handle
Dust Bag
Lock Pin
Bevel Scale
Lower Blade Guard
Base
Detent Override
Miter Lock Knob
Sliding Fence
Table
Miter Scale
Detents
Miter Detent Lever

CUTTING CAPACITIES

The cutting capacity of a miter saw will vary greatly according to the type of saw. Chop and miter saws can typically cut through a 2×6 in terms of width. The maximum depth of cut will depend on the type of guard that the saw employs. Most saws can handle a 4×4. Sliding compound saws have a greater width capacity, commonly 10" to 12"; check the manufacturer's specifications if you're in doubt.

When it comes to describing a miter saw's maximum cutting capacities, manufacturers typically list four categories: maximum cut at 90 degrees, maximum cut at 45 degrees, maximum cut at a 45-degree bevel, and the maximum compound cut that the saw is capable of making. See the chart on the opposite page for generic cutting capacities of the three types of miter saws.

Maximum cut at 90 degrees. A miter saw can cut through the largest workpiece at its most basic when the blade is at 90 degrees to the fence and table, as shown in the photo above. The original chop saw could handle a 2×4. Modern sliding compound miter saws can cut through a 4×12. In many cases manufacturers specify two cuts to define the saw's capabilities—typically, that it can cut through a 2×6 or a 4×4—to describe the widest and thickest workpiece the saw can handle at 90 degrees.

Maximum cut at 45-degree miter. As soon as you angle the blade on a miter saw, you reduce its cutting capacity, as shown in the photo above. That's because you're actually making a longer cut. For example, when you cut a 2×4 at a 45-degree miter, you're actually making a 4.95"-long cut. So a typical 10" compound miter saw that's capable of cutting through a 2×6 at 90 degrees can only cut through a 2×4 at a 45-degree miter angle.

Maximum cut at 45-degree bevel. When you tilt the blade to 45 degrees, as shown in the photo above, you retain the saw's ability to cut the same width workpiece, but you reduce its ability to cut thicker stock. That's because the head of the saw is much closer to the tabletop. A typical 10" compound miter saw that can handle a 2×6 or 4×4 at 90 degrees can bevel-cut a 2×6 but not a 4×4.

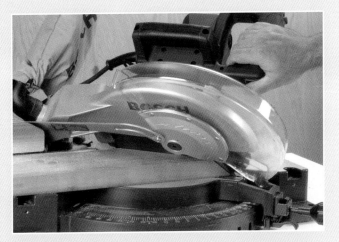

Maximum compound cut. If you pivot a saw to 45 degrees and tilt the blade to 45 degrees, you'll define the saw's maximum compound cut capacity, as shown in the photo above. As a general rule, a saw's compound cutting capacity will be the same as its 45-degree capacity since pivoting the blade will have the greatest impact on reducing cutting capacity. The exception to this is sliding compound saws, where the width capacity is similar, but the thickness-cutting capacity decreases because of the proximity of the tilted blade to the saw's table.

TYPICAL MITER SAW CUTTING CAPACITIES

	10" Chop	10" Compound	10" Sliding Compound
Crosscut	4 x 4 2 x 6	4 x 4 2 x 6	4 x 12 2 x 12
45-degree miter	2 x 4	2 x 4	4 x 8
45-degree bevel	n/a	2 x 6	2 x 12
Compound cut	n/a	2 x 4	2 x 8

Miter Saw Features

Miter saws are classified in two ways: type and blade size. The three types are: miter saw, compound miter saw, and sliding compound miter saw, as described on pages 8–10.

Blade size

Along with the type of saw, the blade size is listed when describing the saw, as in a 10" sliding compound miter saw. Blade diameters vary from $7\frac{1}{2}$" up to 12", with 10" being the most common. In general, the larger the blade diameter, the greater the cutting capacity of the saw. This pertains mainly to compound miter saws, since the only way to increase cutting capacity is to increase the diameter of the blade. Not so with a sliding compound saw, as the sliding carriage increases the crosscutting capacity of the saw (not its thickness-cutting capacity). For more on the cutting capacity of the various types of miter saws, see pages 12–13.

Motor rating

Unlike most stationary power tools, where motor ratings are specified in horsepower, virtually all miter saw motors are rated in amperes. This is by far the truest indicator of how capable the tool is of performing its tasks. As a general rule of thumb, the higher the amperage, the more powerful the motor. Amperage ratings can be found on the motor label, as shown in the middle photo. The vast majority of the miter saws currently on the market employ a 15-amp motor.

Drive type

There are two types of drives used to power the blade of a miter saw: gear-drive and belt-drive. With a gear-drive saw, the motor shaft meshes with a set of gears that turn the saw arbor. On a belt-drive saw (bottom photo), the motor shaft turns a belt, which in turn drives the saw arbor. Both work well, but gear-drive systems tend to be more reliable, as there's no risk of belt slippage.

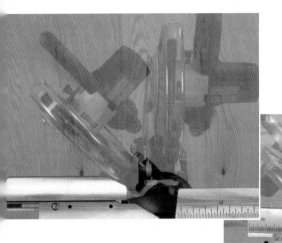

Bevel tilt

Although you may not think it's a big deal, a saw that tilts in both directions can save you a lot of headaches trying to figure out how to make a cut, especially a compound miter. Miter saws that bevel-tilt in only one direction are still more common than saws that tilt in both directions. That's because dual-tilt saws are more expensive, and most woodworkers and DIY'ers can make do with a single-tilt saw. If you're planning on installing a lot of molding, consider spending the extra for a dual-tilt saw. It really can prevent a lot of frustration, along with saving you money in the long run (in terms of buying replacement molding when you make a wrong cut—crown molding in particular is quite expensive).

Miter scale and bevel scales

Since you constantly pivot and angle the blade of your miter saw, it's important that both the miter and bevel scales be easy to read. This has to do both with the actual numbers and indicator lines as well as the indicator itself. For instance, look at the difference between the scales in the two photos at near left. The scale on the upper saw is easy to read and has plenty of room between indicator lines to judge, say, the halfway point. The scale on the miter saw in the lower photo is condensed and hard to read. It may seem like a small detail, but it's not when you want to dial in to $43^1/_2$ degrees.

DIGITAL READOUTS

One way to prevent errors when reading scales is to replace the scales with a digital readout. That's exactly what Hitachi did in the saw shown in the photo below. An easy-to-read digital display takes the guesswork out of hitting just the right angle.

Miter detents

All miter saws have some form of detent system that allows you to quickly—and hopefully, accurately—lock into the more common angles you'll want to cut at. Typical detents are located at 90 degrees, 45 degrees, and $22^1/_2$ degrees. Other detents may be provided for cutting crown molding. Since you'll be pivoting a saw constantly and using these detents, it's important that they be easy to use and lock in positively. Also, since you'll frequently want to cut just a hair to one side of a detent, look for a saw with a detent override, like the Bosch saw shown in the middle left photo. A detent override lets you pivot the blade at any angle. Without one it's difficult to lock the blade in at an angle that's close to a detent, as the detent tries to pull the blade over to its preset angle.

Bevel detents

Any miter saw that tilts has a pair of bevel stops: one at 0 degrees and the other at 45 degrees. As with miter detents, these stops should be easy to use and positive. But unlike detents, they should also be adjustable. Although most miter saws don't have detents on the bevel scale, some offer a detent or two for cutting crown molding, like the 12" Bosch saw shown in the middle right photo. It has a push-in detent to set the blade tilt precisely at 33.9 degrees for cutting crown.

Fixed fences

Every miter saw has a set of fixed fences, one on each side of the blade, to provide an accurate reference point for making a cut. The fence is generally milled or cast and serves to present a workpiece perpendicular to the blade (bottom left photo). The higher the fence, the more surface area it offers, which is useful when cutting thick stock. Most fences have holes or slots near the bottom for attaching a wood auxiliary fence or stop. Look for fixed fences that are machined smooth, and take a small engineer's square with you when shopping for a miter saw to check that the fence is perfectly 90 degrees to the tabletop.

Sliding fences

As soon as manufacturers started to tilt the blade on a miter saw—and create compound miter saws—they had to do something about the fixed fences. That's because they get in the way of the motor head and blade when you make a bevel cut. To get around this, they developed sliding fences like the one shown in the bottom right photo. The idea is simple: The upper fence slides in a groove in the lower fixed fence and can be slid out of the way for a bevel cut and locked in place. If you plan on making a lot of bevel cuts, it's important that the sliding fence or fences operate smoothly and with minimal effort. On some saws, the sliding fence has to be removed to make a bevel cut. Not a big deal for an occasional cut, but rather annoying for frequent bevel cuts.

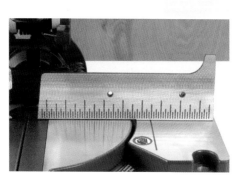

Blade guard

The blade guard is the most important safety device on a miter saw. It should cover the blade and retract only to make the cut. A blade guard should protect your fingers while still affording an optimum view of the cut. Blade guards vary wildly from one manufacturer to another, and finding one that works for you really requires getting your hands on the various saws. We prefer the clear plastic guard like the one shown in the Bosch saw in the top left photo, as it offers the best view of the cut.

Electric brakes

Virtually all miter saws now come standard with an electric brake. Some older saws didn't have this feature, and the saw blade would continue to spin even after the power was off—not a safe situation. Electric brakes remove this safety hazard by quickly stopping the saw shortly after the cut has been made. Once the cut is finished and the switch is released, a secondary set of coils pulse the motor in the reverse direction for a split second. This essentially takes out 80% to 90% of the blade's momentum, causing it to come to a complete stop in 2 to 3 seconds.

Shaft lock

Blade changing on a miter saw is simplified if the saw has a shaft lock to keep the blade from turning as you loosen the arbor nut. In most cases, the shaft lock is a push button located on the side of the motor housing, as shown in the photo above left. The shaft lock should be readily accessible and not require excessive force to hold it in place for blade changing.

Wing extensions

Many miter saws now come with wing extensions to help stabilize long cuts. There is a variety of wing extensions available, ranging from simple tubular bars to cast-aluminum tables like those shown on the Bosch miter saw in the bottom photo. We prefer the table-style extensions, as we've found that they offer better support.

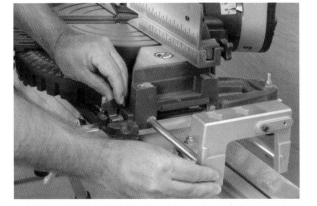

Adjustable kerf inserts

The table on all miter saws is grooved directly under the blade so that the blade doesn't cut into its surface. On the original chop saws, this groove was often fairly narrow to closely hug the blade. Hugging the blade like this supported the underside of the workpiece as the blade passed through it and helped to reduce splintering. But as soon as manufacturers starting tilting the blade for a bevel cut, they had to widen this groove to keep the angled blade from cutting into the tabletop. Widening the groove removes the support under the workpiece, and so splintering became an issue. The solution they came up with is a set of adjustable inserts that fit in the groove in the tabletop as shown in the middle photo. For standard cuts, the inserts are moved in close to the blade and when you need to bevel, the inserts can be slid apart as needed. (For more on splinter-free cuts, see page 138.)

Dust bags/collection

Like any power saw, a miter saw is capable of producing copious amounts of sawdust. That's why virtually every miter saw has some sort of provision for dust collection or removal. At the very least, a saw will have a dust port that hooks up to a chute positioned directly behind the saw blade (bottom right photo). The gullets of the blade throw the dust back into the chute, where it either gets sucked up by a shop vacuum (or dust collection system) or empties into a dust bag. Most woodworkers make do with a dust bag, as hooking up a miter saw to flexible hose creates problems when you pivot the saw to make a cut. As with any other feature, how well a saw collects dust varies from one saw maker to another. Of the saws we've used over the years, we've found the dust collecting capabilities of the saws that Makita makes to be a cut above the rest.

Hold-downs

Another feature to look for is built-in hold-downs. These are basically clamps that attach to the fence or body of the saw and press a workpiece flat against the table or fence (bottom left photo). This not only adds precision, but it also prevents dangerous situations from occurring when either side of a long board that's cut tilts up into the blade after a cut is made. Unless you've got three hands, you can't hold down both pieces and make the cut at the same time—a hold-down serves as your third hand.

LASER GUIDES

In our opinion, laser guides are one of the niftier new features that have been added to miter saws in recent years. A laser guide shoots a red laser beam directly onto the workpiece to accurately show where the blade will cut. This accessory has become so popular that many new saws come with laser guides installed as standard. Not to worry, though, if you have an older saw: A number of saw and accessory manufacturers sell laser upgrade kits. Laser guides can shoot a single or dual beam and are either turned on and off via a switch or automatically turned on when the blade reaches a set rpm.

Single-beam laser. With a single-beam laser, the laser beam directed onto the workpiece can be adjusted to define either the right or left side of the blade, as shown in the top photo. Alternatively, some single-laser guides shoot a 1/8"-wide beam to define the full width of the blade.

Dual-beam laser. On a dual-beam laser guide, two separate beams are directed onto the workpiece to define the edges of the blade, as shown in the middle photo. Most woodworkers prefer this setup, as there's no question where the blade will make its cut and where the cut-off or waste begins.

Operation. How the laser guide operates will depend on the manufacturer. Some laser guides are turned on and off by a separate switch, like the one shown on the Hitachi saw in the photo at left. The advantage of this type of guide is that the beam can be on without the saw blade spinning. Other laser guides only come on once the blade reaches a set rpm (typically 500 rpm). This means you have to energize the saw to light the laser and align your cut. Either system works well, but both take some getting used to.

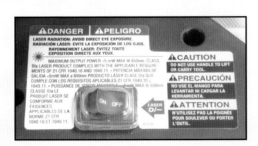

■ LASER SAFETY

Just because the laser in a miter saw laser guide is small doesn't mean it can't be harmful. Laser radiation can hurt you. Make sure to heed the manufacturer's warnings and never stare directly into the beam, as it can—and will—damage your eyes.

Ergonomics

We always recommend that tool shoppers get their hands on a potential tool before buying it. This is the only way to determine whether the tool's ergonomics and your hands are a good match. Grip the tool, turn the power switch on and off, pivot and tilt the saw blade, etc. There are two ergonomic features that will greatly affect how comfortable any given miter saw is for you to use: the saw handle type and location, and the miter handle that's used to pivot the blade. Virtually every time you use your miter saw you'll be operating both of these controls.

Saw handle

There are two main features to look for in a saw handle: how the handle is oriented, and the location and ease of use of the built-in power switch. Handle orientation is either horizontal (left middle photo) or vertical (right middle photo). We've always found vertical handles to be awkward and extremely fatiguing to use over extended periods of time, such as when framing or trimming out a room. Innovative saw manufacturers like Bosch realize this is a matter of personal preference and have designed their handles to be adjustable in four positions. The location and type of power switch in the handle will also affect how comfortable the saw is for you to use. Most saws have a built-in safety switch that must first be depressed before the blade can be energized. Here again, forward-thinking saw makers have designed handles with safety releases on both sides of the handle, acknowledging that there are right- and left-handed woodworkers out there. A small detail maybe, but it's a big deal if you're a southpaw.

Miter handle

Second only to the main power handle, the miter handle will have a huge impact on how easy or awkward it is to pivot the blade for miter cuts.

Virtually all miter saws use either a handle or knob to lock the pivoting table in place at the desired angle. The big difference is how the detents operate. The two most common detent options are a detent lever that's pushed down from above the handle to disengage the detent (bottom right photo) and a detent lever that's pulled up from below the handle to disengage the detent (bottom left photo). We prefer the detent levers that are pulled up, as they're easier to operate than the push-down style. It's just more natural to pull up and pivot than to push down and pivot. Here again, this is a matter of personal preference. What's important is that the detent lock positively and not move when the miter handle is locked down—a common trait of poor-quality saws. As we mentioned previously, a detent override is an extremely useful feature that makes it easy to lock that saw in place close to a detent angle—something that's near impossible on a saw without an override.

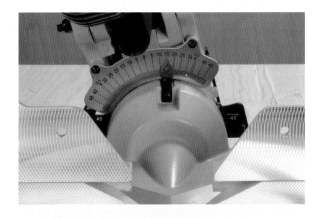

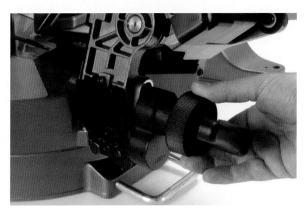

Bevel adjustments

The controls for tilting the blade of a compound miter saw have never been convenient. That's because for the most part, they're located at the rear of the saw, as shown in the top photo. This means that adjusting the bevel is awkward at best. One hand has to reach behind the saw to loosen the adjustment knob or lever while you use your other hand to tilt the motor head/blade. At the same time you have to try to accurately read the bevel scale, which is often quite small. Nevertheless, manufacturers continue to try to make this less awkward. One solution developed by Hitachi and shown in the middle photo is an adjustment knob that tilts the blade from the rear. Alternatively, some manufacturers have moved the tilt controls up to the front of the saw, as described in the sidebar on page 23.

Hold-downs

Acknowledging that safety and accuracy are becoming increasingly important with miter saws, most manufacturers now provide some sort of hold-down with their saws as a standard accessory. Hold-downs fit into holes or slots in the saw base and are used to press a workpiece firmly into the surface of the saw table. This keeps long workpieces from tilting up dangerously at the end of a cut, and it also prevents the workpiece from "creeping" or shifting during a cut to ensure a more accurate cut. Hold-downs vary significantly from one saw maker to another. Versions range from easy-to-use models that can be operated with one hand (bottom left photo) to less convenient versions that require both hands to set up and adjust, as shown in the bottom right photo.

Blade guard

As we mentioned on page 17, you want a blade guard that operates smoothly while affording the best view of the workpiece. In terms of safety, you also want a blade guard that protects you from the blade as much as possible. Try this test: Pull the head of the miter saw all the way down until it hits the depth limit. Than look at the front of the saw to see how much blade is exposed. Any blade exposed at all is a potential hazard. Notice the difference between the two 12" compound saws in the top photos.

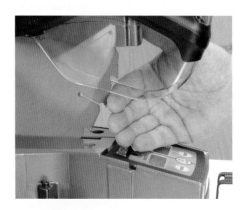

On the saw in the top right photo, 2" to 3" of saw blade is left exposed with the guard fully in place. Compare this to the safer saw in the top left photo. Here the blade guard completely covers the blade, keeping your fingers safe.

Blade changing

Although it may seem like changing the blade on a miter saw would be fairly simple, it gets a bit complicated because of the blade guard. In particular, the linkage that connects the arm of the saw to the blade guard to retract it automatically gets in the way. On some saws this is a minor inconvenience; on others it can be a real hassle. That's why it's a good idea when shopping for a miter saw to either ask a sales associate to show you how to remove and replace a blade or do it yourself. Fortunately, unlike with a table saw, odds are you won't be changing blades frequently. For the most part, you'll keep a quality carbide-tipped crosscut blade in place until it needs cleaning or sharpening.

FINE ADJUSTMENTS

On some of the higher-end miter saws on the market, you'll find some nice additional features like micro-fine adjustments. An example of this is the micro-angle adjust on the Bosch saw shown in the photo at left. It's used by first engaging the detent override. Then the small knob is pushed forward to engage the micro-adjust. Turning the knob will then fine-tune the blade angle in very small increments. Just the thing for tweaking a piece of molding to fit an odd-angle corner.

Movable fences

There are two basic types of movable fences on miter saws: sliding and pivoting. Both are designed to move out of the way when you tilt the saw to make a bevel cut. If the saw only tilts in one direction, the saw will typically only have a single movable fence; dual-tilt saws have two movable fences. Unless you make a lot of bevel cuts, you won't notice much difference between the two. The advantage that the pivoting fence offers (middle right photo) is it quickly pivots out of the way and no adjustment is necessary. Sliding fences (middle left photo) have a lock-down knob of some sort that must be loosened and then retightened to move the fence out of the way and lock it in its new position. Here again, not a big deal unless you're making a lot of bevel cuts, where you may find the pivoting-style fence to be more convenient.

Carrying handle

With a miter saw weighing in at upwards of 60 pounds, it's no wonder that the manufacturers add carrying handles to their saws. In addition to making the saw easier to carry around, the main reason they add the handle is so that you won't try to carry the saw by its main operating handle. Don't be tempted to lift the saw by this handle, as it's easy to damage the saw and torque it out of alignment. When shopping for a saw, pick it up by the carrying handle to see how truly portable it is. Look for a handle that's centered on the weight and bulk of the saw, as shown in the bottom left photo. Avoid saws where the handle is off-center and makes it hard to balance the saw, as shown in the bottom right photo. If a saw's weight is a problem, consider buying or building a portable stand like those shown on page 32.)

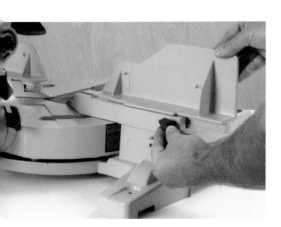

UP-FRONT CONTROLS

In an effort to make operating the controls of a miter saw more convenient, a number of saw makers have brought the bevel controls up to the front of the saw, as shown in the photo below. This eliminates the awkward reaching, positioning, and tightening required with saws that have bevel controls in the rear of the saw.

■ RECOMMENDATIONS

If you can afford it, consider buying two miter saws: a small lightweight compound miter saw for on-site work (the Bosch cordless saw is perfect for this) and a sliding compound miter saw for the shop. Although dual-tilt is a great feature, unless you're installing a lot of molding, you can likely live without this cost-adding feature. If money is tight, go with a quality compound saw. Look for smooth castings and easy-to-use adjustments. Tilt and rotate the blade to make sure it slides and pivots easily and locks securely in place once the knobs are tightened. Also, be on the lookout for package deals. Manufacturers often sweeten the deal by throwing in extras. A quality carbide-tipped blade is an excellent bonus, as these can easily cost over $100.

CHOP SAWS

Plain miter or chop saws are becoming increasingly harder to find, as they've all but been replaced with the more versatile compound miter saws. If you're looking for an inexpensive shop saw that will be used primarily for breaking down lumber into shorter lengths, look no further than a chop saw. One of their biggest advantages—their simplicity—is also their biggest limitation. On the plus side: Because they have fewer moving parts, these small saws tend to stay accurate longer compared to their more complex cousins.

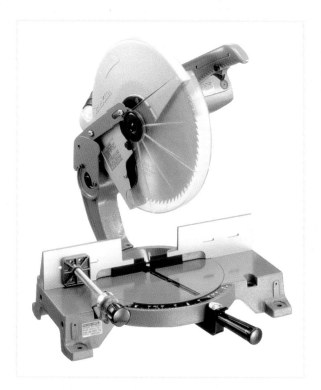

CHOP SAWS

Model	Blade	Motor	Tilt	Brake	Laser	Crosscut	45° Miter	Weight
B&D BT100	10"	15-amp	No	Yes	No	4×4 2×6	2×4	28 lbs.
Hitachi	10"	13-amp	No	Yes	No	4×4	2×4 2×6	27 lbs.
Makita LS1030	10"	15-amp	No	Yes	No	$2^3/_4 \times 5^1/_8$"	2×4	24 lbs.
Milwaukee	10"	15-amp	No	Yes	No	4×4 2×6	2×4	37 lbs.

■ RECOMMENDATIONS

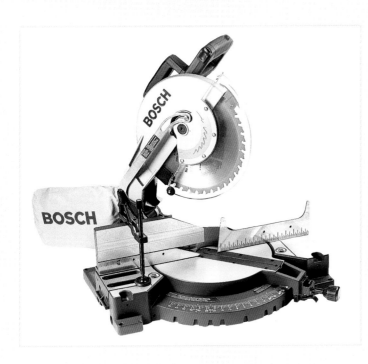

COMPOUND MITER SAWS

When it comes time to narrow down choices when shopping for a compound miter saw, the two things to really pay close attention to are features and ergonomics. Since virtually all miter saws use the same 15-amp motor, power isn't a concern. Any reasonable-quality saw will be able to cut through any lumber you plan on working with. So it really boils down to what features are important to you.

If you plan on installing molding,— particularly crown—consider investing in a dual-tilt saw. This extra feature will cost you more, but will save you considerable headache when installing moldings later. We also feel a detent override is an essential feature in a miter saw, as most walls aren't plumb and you'll frequently need to tweak an angle to get molding to fit. We've also become quite accustomed to using a miter saw with a laser guide. No, it's not absolutely essential, but once you've used a miter saw with a laser guide, it sure is tough going back to a non-laser saw.

(continued)

■ RECOMMENDATIONS

COMPOUND MITER SAWS *(continued)*

COMPOUND MITER SAWS

Model	Blade	Motor	Tilt	Brake	Laser	Crosscut	45° Miter	45° Bevel	Compound	Weight
B&D FS1500	10"	15-amp	L	Yes	No	$4 \times 4/2 \times 6$	2×4	2×6	2×4	30 lbs.
Bosch 3912	12"	15-amp	L	Yes	No	$4 \times 6/3 \times 8$	$4 \times 4/2 \times 8$	3×6	3×4	43 lbs.
Bosch 4212	12"	15-amp	L/R	Yes	No	2×8	4×4	R: 2×6 L: 2×8	4×4	46 lbs.
Bosch 4212L	12"	15-amp	L/R	Yes	Yes	2×8	4×4	R: 2×6 L: 2×8	4×4	46 lbs.
Craftsman 21203	10"	15-amp	L	No	No	2×6	2×6	2×6	2×6	46 lbs.
Craftsman 21215	12"	15-amp	L	Yes	Yes	$2^{1}/_{2}" \times 7^{7}/_{8}"$	$2^{1}/_{2}" \times 6"$	2×8	2×6	49 lbs.
Craftsman 21235	12"	15-amp	L	Yes	Yes	$4 \times 4/2 \times 8$	2×6	2×6	2×4	50 lbs.
Delta MS250	10"	13.3-amp	L	Yes	No	$4 \times 4/2 \times 6$	2×4	2×6	2×4	28 lbs.
Delta MS265	10"	15-amp	L	Yes	No	$2^{3}/_{4}" \times 5^{5}/_{8}"$	2×4	2×6	2×4	33 lbs.
Delta 36-585	10"	15-amp	L/R	Yes	No	$4 \times 4/3 \times 6$	$2^{3}/_{8}" \times 4^{1}/_{8}"$	L: 2×6 R: 1×6	L: 2×4 R: 1×4	35 lbs.
Delta MS450	12"	15-amp	L	Yes	No	$4 \times 6/2 \times 8$	2×6	2×6	2×8	53 lbs.
Delta 36-255L	12"	15-amp	L/R	Yes	Yes	$2 \times 8/1 \times 6$	3×6	L: 3×6 2×8	2×6	63 lbs.
Delta 36-312	12"	15-amp	L	Yes	No	$2 \times 8/1 \times 6$	3×6	L: 3×6 2×8	2×6	51 lbs.
Delta 36-412	12"	15-amp	L/R	Yes	No	$4 \times 6/2 \times 10$	$3 \times 4/3 \times 6$	L: 2×10	2×6	56 lbs.
DeWalt DW703	10"	15-amp	L	Yes	No	$4 \times 4/2 \times 6$	2×4	2×6	2v4	33 lbs.
DeWalt DW705S	12"	15-amp	L	Yes	No	$4 \times 6/2 \times 8$	4×4	$4 \times 4/2 \times 6$	4×4	40 lbs.
DeWalt DW706	12"	15-amp	L/R	Yes	No	$4 \times 4/2 \times 8$	$4 \times 4/2 \times 6$	2×8	$4 \times 4/2 \times 6$	44 lbs.
Hitachi C10FCB	10"	15-amp	L	Yes	No	$4 \times 4/2 \times 6$	2×4	2×6	2×4	31 lbs.
Hitachi C10FCH	10"	15-amp	L	Yes	Yes	$4 \times 4/2 \times 6$	2×4	2×6	2×4	28 lbs.
Hitachi CL12LCH	12"	15-amp	L	Yes	Yes	$4 \times 6/2 \times 8$	2×6	2×8	2×6	42 lbs.
Makita LS1040	10"	15-amp	L	Yes	No	2×6	2×6	2×6	2×4	24 lbs.
Makita LS1221	12"	15-amp	L	Yes	No	4×6	4×4	2×6	2×6	36 lbs.
Milwaukee 6494-6	10"	15-amp	L	Yes	No	$4 \times 4/2 \times 6$	2×4	2×6	2×4	38 lbs.
PC 3700L	10"	15-amp	L	Yes	Yes	$4 \times 4/2 \times 6$	$4 \times 4/2 \times 4$	2×4	2×4	40 lbs.
PC 3802L	12"	15-amp	L	Yes	Yes	2×8	2×6	2×8	4×4	63 lbs.

■ RECOMMENDATIONS

SLIDING COMPOUND MITER SAWS

Since the motor power and cutting capacities of most sliding compound miter saws are similar, choosing a saw boils down to features, ergonomics, and price. As with a compound miter saw, we like the dual-tilt feature as well as a laser guide. Other than that, you really need to get your hands on the saws to find the one that's the most comfortable for you that has the features you want. Alternatively, check out your local woodworkers' club or woodworkers' chat room (like www.theoak.com) for other woodworkers' views on specific types and brands of miter saws.

SLIDING COMPOUND MITER SAWS

Model	Blade	Motor	Tilt	Brake	Laser	Crosscut	45° Miter	45° Bevel	Compound	Weight
Bosch 3915	10"	13-amp	L	Yes	No	4×12	4×8	2×12	2×8	47 lbs.
Bosch 4410L	10"	15-amp	L/R	Yes	Yes	4×12	2×12	2×8	1×8	55 lbs.
Bosch 5412L	12"	15-amp	L/R	Yes	Yes	4×12	4×8	2×12	2×8	59 lbs.
DeWalt DW712	8½"	15-amp	L	Yes	No	2×12	2×8	2×12	2×8	43 lbs.
DeWalt DW708	12"	15-amp	L/R	Yes	No	4×12	4×8	2×12	2×12	57 lbs.
Hitachi C10FSH	10"	12-amp	L/R	Yes	Yes	4×12	4×8	2×12	2×8	43 lbs.
Hitachi 12FSA	12"	12-amp	L/R	Yes	No	4×12	4×8	2×12	2×8	55 lbs.
Makita LS0714	7½"	10-amp	L	Yes	No	2×12	2×8	2×12	2×8	28 lbs.
Makita LS1011N	10"	13-amp	L	Yes	No	2×12	2×8	2×12	2×8	38 lbs.
Makita LS1013	10"	13-amp	L/R	Yes	No	4×12	2×8	2×12	2×8	47 lbs.
Makita LS1214	12"	15-amp	L/R	Yes	No	4×12	4×8	2×12	2×8	53 lbs.
Milwaukee 6497-6	10"	15-amp	L	Yes	No	4×12	4×8	2×10	2×8	56 lbs.
Porter-Cable 3807	10"	15-amp	L	Yes	No	4×12	2×8/4×4	2×12	2×8	57 lbs.

2 Miter Saw Accessories

For the most part, a miter saw is pretty much ready to go right out of the box. You don't need to buy a bunch of fancy accessories for it to do its job well. There are, however, a few accessories that you might find make it easier to use. These include blades that can handle a variety of materials, stands that position the saw at the correct working height while supporting even long workpieces, auxiliary fences that help you make accurate repeat cuts, wing extensions to stabilize and support your cuts, jigs for cutting crown molding, and laser guides to show you exactly where the cut will be made. In this chapter, we'll cover all of these accessories and more. We'll help you decide which if any you need, and more importantly, what to look for when you decide to buy.

There are a few accessories for the miter saw that can improve its performance. These include blades, stands, and after-market fences.

Blades

The number one accessory for a miter saw is the saw blade. Blades are available in diameters ranging from $7\frac{1}{2}$" up to 12", with 10" being the most common. The hole in the center of the saw that fits over the saw arbor is typically $\frac{5}{8}$" in diameter, although other sizes are used.

Blade types

There are numerous types of saw blades available, but only one type that is really suitable for the miter saw—the crosscut blade. The teeth on a crosscut blade are usually alternate-tooth bevel (see the tooth configuration drawing on the opposite page)—and there are a lot of them, as shown in the middle photo. Typical tooth count on a quality crosscut blade will vary from 60 to 80 teeth. The hook angle is usually around 2 degrees to create a slicing cut. The higher-tooth-count blades will produce a virtually chip-free cut that will be satin smooth.

Blade materials

There are two main materials used to make saw blades: high-speed steel (HSS) and carbide. With a HSS blade, the entire blade is made of high-speed steel (top photo). But these blades tend to dull quickly, so saw blade manufacturers weld carbide tips onto the teeth. As far as we're concerned, the majority of the HSS blades out there are best used for shop clocks. Carbide-tipped is the only way to go. The only advantage a HSS steel blade offers (besides being cheaper) is that it's less expensive to sharpen. But this is offset by the frequent number of sharpenings the blade will need. That is carbide's big claim to fame—a carbide-tipped blade will stay sharper a whole lot longer than HSS—and it can be resharpened as well (just make sure you use a sharpening service that's experienced with carbide). The quality of the blade will have much to do with the thickness and quality of the carbide, so go with a name you can trust.

It's important to know that a quality carbide-tipped crosscut blade (middle photo) can easily cost over $100. But as long as you keep it away from metal

fasteners, it'll last a long time. That's why we don't recommend cutting used lumber with this blade—or with a miter saw, for that matter. Fit a demolition blade on a circular saw and use that instead.

Tooth configurations

Miter saw blades are available in numerous profiles and configurations. You can get blades designed just for coarse work (few teeth, flat top grind) or cross-cutting (many teeth, ATB grind), or a combination blade (typically ATB with a raker tooth), as illustrated in the drawing on page 31. Triple chip and flat grind is another popular choice for combination blades. A typical 10" crosscut blade will sport 60 teeth; a 12" blade typically has 80 teeth. As a general rule of thumb, the more teeth, the smoother the cut. But there's a downside to so many teeth. The more teeth, the more friction is created, which means a quality crosscut blade can heat up in a hurry. That's why many saw blade manufacturers machine expansion slots in the perimeter of the blade. When the blade heats up and expands, these slots allow the blade to maintain its shape.

The most common tooth configuration for a crosscut blade is the ATB grind. That is, the tops of alternating teeth are beveled in the opposite direction. This creates knife-like points which are essential to cleanly cut across the grain. The steeper this angle, the more of a scoring action is produced and the cleaner the cut. Saw blade manufacturers are constantly tinkering with the top bevel angle along with the hook angle—the angle on the front face of the tooth—searching for the ultimate cutoff blade. On a table saw blade, the hook angle is fairly positive—the teeth lean forward to create a fairly aggressive cut. On miter saw blades, the hook angle is low because they don't want the blade to grab the workpiece. Some miter saw blades even sport a negative hook angle—they actually lean backwards. But a low hook angle means that the saw motor needs to work harder to make the cut. It's no wonder there are so many variations of miter saw blades on the market. Look for blades with ATB teeth, a low or negative hook angle, and quality carbide—and stick with a name you can trust (we use Freud blades in our shop).

BLADE TOOTH CONFIGURATIONS

TRIPLE CHIP & FLAT GRIND

ATB & RAKER

FLAT TOP GRIND

ATB

HIGH-TECH BLADES

Advances in saw blade technology by cutting-edge manufacturers have improved performance of carbide-tipped blades tremendously. Two common advances are expansion slots and anti-vibration slots cut into the body of the blade. Expansion slots reduce noise and allow the blade to expand and contract as needed as it heats in use. Anti-vibration slots reduce vibration and chatter.

Stands

Although woodworkers and DIY'ers frequently mount their miter saw to a workbench or other cabinet in their shop, it's not very convenient when they need to use the saw on site. A number of tool manufacturers make stands for miter saws. These range from simple fold-up stands to elaborate units with built-in fences and stops. Costs range from $150 to over $300. If you do a lot of on-site work, one of these may be a good investment. If not, you can always clamp the saw to a sawhorse. Alternatively, if you don't want to spend the money on a stand, consider building your own.

Simple stands

Inexpensive stands don't do much more than hold and position your miter saw at a convenient height, as shown in the photo at right. Generally, this style of stand will have simple extensions on both sides of the saw to support long stock. These extensions may or may not have built-in length stops. The advantage to a simple stand is it's inexpensive, lightweight, and highly portable. On the downside, they don't hold up well to heavy-duty use. If you only occasionally need to work on site, consider one of these lightweight simple stands.

Deluxe stands

Deluxe stands like the Bosch miter saw stand shown in the bottom photo are built to handle heavy-duty use. The body and legs of the stand are stout extruded aluminum. The legs snap quickly into place, and one leg is adjustable to compensate for an uneven floor. Extension rails on both sides of the saw are adjustable and extend out to support even the longest lumber. Adjustable length stops

attach to both rails to make duplicating parts a breeze. Although this beefy stand is fairly heavy, Bosch added a pair of wheels to one end to make it easy to roll the stand around once it is folded up.

Shop-made stands

Miter saw stands can be pricey, and if you like the idea of one but don't want to spend the money—build your own. The shop-made miter saw stand shown in the photo below offers wing extensions on both sides of the saw, a convenient drawer for storing blades, etc., and a lower bin for cutoffs. Complete step-by-step instructions for this stand can be found on pages 92–105.

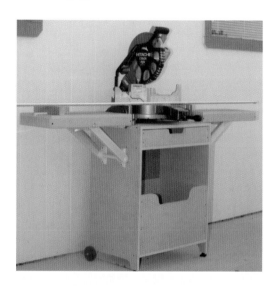

Auxiliary Fences

Since miter saws were originally designed to be used on site by carpenters, it was important that they be as lightweight and portable as possible. This meant a small table and short fences. Modern miter saws are still designed with this in mind. Unfortunately, short tables and fences make it difficult to cut long stock with any kind of accuracy. That's why many saw and accessory manufacturers offer auxiliary fences for their saws. Auxiliary fence systems can be simple or elaborate—you can even make your own; see below.

Woodhaven fence

There are a number of after-market fence systems you can add to your saw to increase its performance. The Contractor Kit manufactured by Woodhaven (www.woodhaven.com) and shown in the top photo includes two 24" machined Ultra Track fences that mount to the front of your chop saw fence, but are easily removed for transport. The system includes a curved stop, a straight stop, and a track/table extension. Although this system requires that you drill mounting holes in your chop saw fence, Woodhaven also sells a no-drill option. The track/table extension provides support for long boards and increases the working length of the fence. You supply the $^3/_4$"-thick stock for the desired extension length. This system also accepts various Woodhaven accessories, including an angle head that lets you cut 45-degree angles with the saw set at 90 degrees, or cut tapers by angling the saw slightly. It also accepts a crown jig that positions and holds moldings at the correct angles so all you have to do is make a miter cut—there's no need to fuss with bevel angles. (For more on installing an auxiliary fence, see pages 142–143.)

Biesemeyer fence

Another fence system shown in the middle photo is made by Biesemeyer (www.biesemeyer.com) and is designed to fit most 10" and 12" miter saws. Their table system is available in a variety of lengths (4', 6', and 8') and has a built-in sawdust slot to eliminate buildup problems, which can affect accuracy. Note that you'll most likely need to modify your existing work surface in order to mount the fences so they're flush with your saw table.

Shop-made fence

You can also build your own auxiliary fence. The system shown in the bottom photo and described on pages 110–115 can be made in an afternoon and features a sliding length stop and extension rod for cutting short stock.

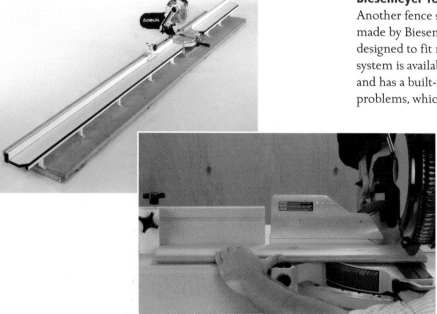

Table Extensions

As we mentioned on page 33, miter saws have always been designed with short tables and fences to promote portability. You can remedy the short fence problem with an auxiliary fence, as described on page 33. But what about the short table? The table is what supports the workpiece, and long workpieces are a real challenge to cut accurately on a short table. Early on in miter saw development, saw makers started offering table extensions to alleviate this problem. Although these do help, they are still not long enough to support long stock well. For this you really need a stand like one of those described on page 32.

Commercial extensions

Most of the commercially available table extensions are similar to those shown in the bottom photos. The two basic types are the single bent rod and the separate rods with end cap. The simplest design is the single bent rod (left saw below). Here a rod is bent in a U-shape to fit into a pair of holes in the saw base. The end of the U is bent up to align with the tabletop. For added portability, the rod can be slid into the base. The other common design (middle and right saws below) offers a more stable platform at the end to better support the workpiece. Table extensions like these are still available as acces-

sories, but most saw makers now include them as standard equipment on their saws.

Shop-made extensions

A shop-made table extension like the one shown in the middle photo is easy to make from scrap lumber. The only real challenge is making them so they end up perfectly flush with your saw table. This often has less to do with the extensions and more to do with the surface they rest on. The most reliable way to make them flush is to make the extensions slightly shorter and then shim them as needed to bring them flush with your saw table. Note that applying a layer of plastic laminate to the top of the extensions will make it easy to slide a workpiece around when aligning it for a cut.

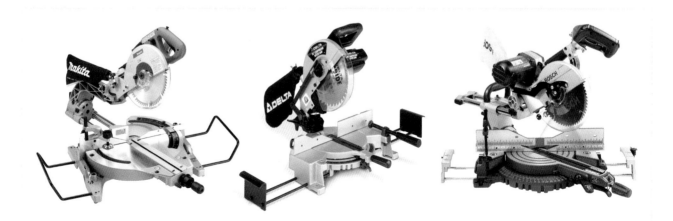

Crown Molding Accessories

Crown molding has a well-deserved reputation for being a pain to cut and install. Even if you can handle the mental gymnastics, simply holding the molding itself in place on the saw can be a challenge (for more on cutting crown, see pages 68–73). With this in mind, most saw manufacturers and a number of accessory makers have developed crown molding stops or crown molding jigs.

Add-on stops

The most common type of aid for cutting crown molding is add-on stops like those shown in the top photo and manufactured by Bosch to fit their saws. The stop is basically a bracket with a lip on the end to hold the crown molding in place. It attaches to the side of the saw base as shown, and adjusts in and out to hold a variety of molding widths. This type of stop is simple but effective.

Crown molding jigs

There are a number of crown molding jigs on the market. The jig manufactured by Bench Dog Tools (www.benchdog.com) shown in the top middle photo holds the molding at its intended angle while you cut it. No more compound cuts and tedious trial and error. Their Crown-Cut jig requires only a simple 45-degree miter cut that any miter saw can do. Woodhaven's crown jig (www.woodhaven.com) attaches to their fence system (see page 33). It also holds molding at the correct angle so all you have to do is make a miter cut (lower middle photo). No need to fuss with bevel angles—and it works on either side of the blade.

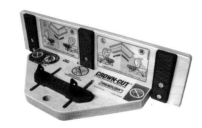

BUILT-IN CROWN STOPS

Since cutting crown and other molding is such a common task for the miter saw, some manufacturers have added built-in stops to their saws, like the Delta saw shown in the photo below. These built-in stops are easy to use—and always right at hand. Just turn the adjustment knob until the stop is roughly positioned. Then lift up the stop until the ears on each side of the stop pop into place. Insert the molding and adjust the stop until the molding is held at the desired angle.

Length Stops

The most reliable way to cut multiple workpieces to identical length with a miter saw is to use a length stop. When miter saws first hit the market, carpenters frequently screwed a scrap of 1×4 to lengthen the fence and then simply clamped a scrap block to the 1×4 at the desired length. This worked fairly well as long as true precision wasn't required. What would work better would be a stop that slid along the fence and could be locked in place with the turn of a knob. That's exactly what a number of saw and accessory manufacturers have designed.

Virtually all of the commercially available stops are designed to fit proprietary fence systems. Two examples of these are shown in the top two photos. Both of these stops are manufactured and sold by Woodhaven (www.woodhaven.com). The straight stop is fine for most cuts; the curved stop is useful for wide or thick stock. Both feature an indicator that utilizes the built-in measuring tape on Woodhaven's fence system.

DIGITAL PROTRACTOR

If you've ever tried to install molding in your home, you already know that most walls aren't plumb and corners aren't square. The challenge to installing molding then is to identify the actual angles where walls and ceilings meet. Bosch recently introduced the perfect partner for a miter saw—the Miterfinder digital protractor shown here. This nifty tool is actually four tools in one: an angle finder, a compound cut calculator, a protractor, and a level. The angle finder will determine the exact angle needed, totally eliminating any guesswork. You simply butt one leg of the protractor on adjacent surfaces and the digital readout tells you the exact angle, as shown in the photo above. The compound cut calculator automatically determines the exact miter and bevel settings necessary to make the molding fit perfectly. There's even a hold function that will freeze measurements until you can get back to your saw. All in all, a whole lot of problem-solving tools in a small package.

Clamps and Hold-Downs

Although many miter saw manufacturers include a clamp or hold-down as a standard accessory for their saws, some don't. With less-expensive saws, you may have to purchase them separately. We feel that clamps and hold-downs not only add precision to your cuts, but they also make them safer, too.

Smooth rod hold-downs

By far the most common type of hold-down is the style shown in the top photo; it has a smooth rod that fits into a hole or holes in the saw base. With this type of hold-down, the rod is locked in place in the hole with a threaded knob. This means that if you want to remove the hold-down, or adjust its position, you first need to loosen the threaded knob. Typically you can raise or lower the hold-down as needed before re-tightening the threaded knob. The downside to this—and it's not a major thing—is that adjusting or removing the hold-down requires you to use both hands.

Knurled rod hold-downs

On the other type of hold-down available, the rod is knurled instead of smooth. What this does for you is the roughened surface will grab the interior of the hole in the saw table when you exert clamping pressure on the hold-down. This allows for single-handed operation, which is nice when you're making a lot of cuts. The quick-action hold-down (bottom photo) is the easiest to use, as you can insert or remove the hold-down with one hand and exert clamping pressure by simply squeezing down on the handle. The threaded-knob version (middle photo) can still be inserted and removed with a single hand, but then you have to adjust the knob on top to apply clamping pressure.

Add-On Laser Guides

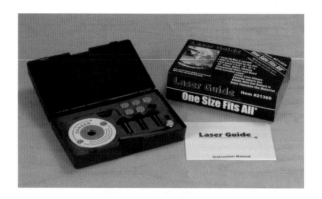

If your miter saw isn't equipped with a laser guide and you want to add this nifty feature, there are a number of accessory manufacturers who make add-on laser guides. The guides shown here are all made by Avenger Products (www.avengerproducts.com). Laser guides are available in single- and dual-beam configurations to fit most saws.

Single-beam

A single-beam laser guide shoots a single line onto your workpiece. On most, you can adjust the guide to mark either the right or left edge of the blade. The guides made by Avenger products are simple to install. All you need to do is replace the outer blade washer with the laser guide unit. No adjustments, no confusing parts; the laser provides you with a visible line for precise cuts. No more guessing exactly where the blade will cut. The laser provides a clean, bright, and easy-to-see beam of light. This style guide has an internal switch that automatically turns on when the saw blade reaches a set rpm (usually 500 rpm) and then turns itself as the blade slows.

Dual-beam

With a dual-beam laser guide, a pair of bright and easy-to-see beams light up both sides of the blade, as shown in the middle photo. No more guessing where the saw blade will cut. This style of laser guide is handy if you tend to cut on both sides of the blade. That is, your waste cuts can be on either the right or left side of the blade. This isn't so easy with a single-line laser guide, as you need to remember which edge of the blade the laser is marking. It's real easy to end up cutting your workpiece $1/8$" too short (the thickness of the blade).

LARGE BORE GUIDES

Avenger also manufacturers a laser guide for saws with large arbors—1" versus 5/8", as shown in the bottom photo. This size guide can be used on some of the larger miter saws.

Dust Collection

When it comes to dust collection on miters saws, there's quite a variety of options available—it all depends on the make and model of the saw. The two most common options are either a dust bag (a provision for hooking up the saw to a shop vacuum), or a dust collector, or both.

Dust bags

Quality dust bags will have some type of internal frame or hanger to keep the bag from sagging closed

as it fills with dust. All have either a zipper or Velcro opening for emptying the bag (left middle photo). It's really surprising how little or much effort some saw makers put into decent dust control. Some saws that are extremely well thought out have poor dust collection abilities, while other saws that are not as well made have great dust control. Go figure. As we mentioned in chapter 1, the only way to find out if the dust bag works is to either cut wood or talk to someone who owns the saw you're interested in. The lack of good dust collection generally has less to do with the bag itself, and more with the funnel or shroud that directs sawdust into the bag.

Hook-ups

On some of the better saws, the dust bag fits onto an elbow that is designed to accept the hose from a standard shop vacuum, as shown in the right middle photo. Hooking up a shop vacuum to your saw will help even a poorly designed saw collect dust better. The only problem is dealing with the hose as you rotate and tilt the saw as you work. The only way to alleviate this situation is to have plenty of slack in the hose so it can reach the limits of your saw's miter and bevel positions.

Shop-made hook-up

If you're fortunate enough to have a dust collection system in your shop, consider making an adapter ring to connect your existing hosing to your miter saw's dust port. The port on most power miter saws is too small for flexible hose. Here's where the adapter ring comes in—it presses onto the port and is sized to accept flexible hose. The adapter ring is made by gluing together two layers of $1/2$" Baltic Birch plywood and then cutting a disk with a circle cutter to fit inside 2" flexible hose. The only tricky part is drilling the inner hole. To do this, hold the plywood disk securely with a hand screw or other clamp and drill the hole carefully with a Forstner bit. Size the hole so it's a press-fit onto the dust port. To attach the ring, press it onto the dust port. If it's too snug, sand the inside with a small drum sander or a dowel wrapped in sandpaper. For a loose fit, wrap a layer or two of masking tape around the port and try again. When you've got a snug fit, slip a hose clamp over a piece of flexible hose and secure the hose to the plywood disk.

SHOP-MADE HOOK-UP

Cut outside diameter to fit inside flex tubing.

Hose Clamp

Exhaust of Miter Saw

Flex Tubing

$3/4$" Plywood Transition Ring

Cut inside diameter to press over exhaust pipe.

3 Basic Miter Saw Techniques

The majority of the cuts you'll make with a miter saw—straight crosscuts and miters—involve the basic techniques laid out in this chapter. Although a miter saw is a fairly straight-forward crosscutting machine, there are important rules to learn regarding safety—as well as correct technique—to ensure that your cuts are precise.

In this chapter we'll start by covering the safety essentials and show you ways to make your saw safer to use. We'll take you through our recommended pre-operation procedure and show you how to set up to make straight crosscuts and miters. There's also information on how to safely and accurately cut long stock, thin stock, wide stock, round stock, and even small pieces—everything you need to know to get started using your compound or sliding compound miter saw.

Miter saws excel at making crosscuts. And the most basic cuts: Straight crosscuts and miters will account for the bulk of the cuts you'll make. Even so, it's important to learn correct technique to ensure accurate and safe cuts.

Miter Saw Safety

As with any power tool, there are rules regarding the safe operation of a miter saw. Most of these are common sense, like keeping your hands away from a spinning blade. But when you're tired or rushed, your common sense or "safety sense" may not be working like it should. There have been so many personal injuries by people disregarding this obvious rule that manufacturers have integrated safety signs directly onto the tables of their saws (as shown in the top photo), hoping to prevent saw owners from making this mistake. To prevent damage to your saw and prevent injuries, read and follow the rules in the sidebar below.

MITER SAW SAFETY RULES

1. Secure the miter saw to a stable supporting surface. Vibration can cause the machine to slide, walk, or tip over and cause an injury.

2. Use only blades of the correct size and type for your saw to prevent damage to the machine or personal injury. Use only crosscut miter saw blades that have a zero-degree or negative hook angle.

3. Make certain that the blade rotates in the correct direction and that the teeth at the bottom of the blade point toward the rear of the saw.

4. Always use the blade guard.

5. Use a sharp, clean blade at all times. Dull and dirty blades can vibrate, causing damage or personal injury.

6. Do not use abrasive cutting wheels on your miter saw. The excess heat and abrasive particles will damage your saw.

7. Always use the kerf plate or inserts; replace if damaged.

8. Tighten the table clamp handle and any other clamps prior to using the saw. Loose clamps can cause parts or the workpiece to be thrown at high speeds.

9. Never start the saw with the blade against the workpiece. The workpiece can be thrown, causing an injury.

10. Keep arms, hands, and fingers away from the blade to prevent injury. Clamp any workpiece to the table that would otherwise place your hand in the table hazard zone.

11. Don't reach underneath the saw unless it is unplugged, as the saw blade is exposed under the saw table.

12. Allow the motor to come to full speed before making the cut. Starting the cut too soon can damage the machine or cause an injury.

13. Never cut ferrous metals or masonry. Either can cause the carbide tips of a blade to fly off the blade at high speeds.

14. Never perform freehand operations. Always hold the work firmly against the fence and table.

15. Properly support long or wide workpieces.

16. Do not allow anyone to stand behind the saw. Cutoffs thrown at high speeds can cause injuries.

17. Read the instruction manual before operating your saw. Learn the machine's application, limitations, and specific hazards.

18. Wear eye and hearing protection. Protect your lungs with a quality dust mask.

19. Maintain your saw in peak condition; keep blades sharp and your saw properly tuned up to prevent injuries.

20. Keep your work area clean. Cluttered areas and benches invite accidents.

21. Never reach in back of the saw blade behind the fence with either hand to hold down or support the workpiece, to remove wood scraps, or for any other reason.

22. Never cross your hand over the intended cut line; supporting the work "cross-handed" (holding the left side of the workpiece with your right hand) is very dangerous.

23. Inspect your workpiece before making a cut; if it's bowed or warped, clamp it with the outside bowed face toward the fence. Always make certain that there is no gap between the workpiece, fence, and table along the line of the cut.

24. Always disconnect the power cord before making any adjustments or attaching any accessories. You may unintentionally start the saw, causing an injury.

ZERO-CLEARANCE FENCE AND TABLE

Zero-clearance fence. You'll notice that many of the rules in the sidebar on the opposite page are concerned with workpieces being thrown at high speeds. The easiest way to prevent this from happening is to add a zero-clearance fence to the fence of your saw. This is nothing more than a scrap of thin plywood or hardboard (at least ¼" thick) that's cut to match the height of your existing fence. The zero-clearance fence can be attached to your existing fence with double-sided carpet tape or, if it's thick enough, with screws driven in through the holes in your fence into the zero-clearance fence, as shown in the top photo. Once it's in place, cut through the fence at the desired angle. Now when you make a cut, the cutoff or waste cannot be thrown backwards—the zero-clearance fence will prevent that.

Zero-clearance table insert. Another hazard referred to in many of the rules in the safety list is caused by dust and chip accumulation under the kerf plate or inserts. There are two different problems that can occur here: A small cutoff can fall into the gap between the inserts and the blade and be thrown off

at high speeds; and dust, chips, or cutoffs can fill in under the kerf plate or inserts and cause the blade to deflect. This not only will ruin your cut, but it can also damage your inserts or kerf plate and could potentially cause an injury.

Just like the zero-clearance fence, you can prevent this potentially hazardous situation from developing by installing a zero-clearance table on top of your existing saw table. Quarter-inch hardboard works great for this. Just cut a piece to match your existing table and fasten it to the fixed table portion (not the pivoting table section) with double-sided carpet tape. Then make a cut at the desired angle as shown in the photo below. The zero-clearance table will "hug" the blade, preventing waste from falling down and interfering with the blade.

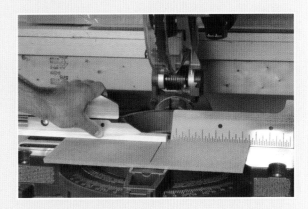

Note that when you install either of the zero-clearance devices described here, you will be reducing the cutting capacity of your saw by ¼"—either the thickness or width capacity, depending on which fence you install (or maybe both fences). Also, if you make a series of angled miter cuts, you may cut wedges out of the fence or table and it will need replacing.

Pre-Use Operations

Every time you go to use your miter saw, it's a good idea to get into the habit of performing a quick pre-use check as described here.

Check the blade

The first thing you should check on your saw is that the blade guard is functioning properly and that the blade is in good shape. Start by gripping the front edge of the guard, and then raise it to make sure the linkage is free; pull down on the main handle to make sure the guard retracts as it should. Return the handle to its upright position and lift up the guard again to expose the blade. Spin the blade manually to check the teeth as shown in the top photo. Look for chipped or missing carbide tips and for any cracks in the blade; replace the blade if you find either of these. Inspect the blade for cleanliness; a dirty blade will vibrate and cause poor cuts and possible injuries (see page 133 for cleaning blades).

Set the miter angle

Once you're sure the blade and guard are in good shape, go ahead and adjust the miter angle as needed. Loosen the miter lock—usually the miter handle—and pivot the saw to the desired angle, as shown in the middle photo. If you're not using one of the built-in detents, make sure to check the angle as described on page 52 before locking the table in at the desired angle by retightening the miter lock handle. If you're making any cut where the blade is 90 degrees to the table, consider doing a quick accuracy test as described in the sidebar on the opposite page before cutting your project parts.

Set the bevel angle

If you're making a bevel cut, adjust the saw to the desired angle. In most cases, this means loosening a bevel lock and then tilting the motor carriage, as shown in the bottom photo, to the desired angle. If you're not using one of the built-in detents or stops, make sure to check the angle as described on page 64 before locking the saw in at the desired angle.

Position the workpiece

With the miter saw adjusted to the desired angles, you can position the workpiece for your cut. Use one of the marking techniques described on page 47 to define the cut line on your workpiece. Then slide the workpiece over until your mark or line is aligned with the blade, as shown in the top photo. If your saw is equipped with a laser guide, this is a snap.

Support the workpiece

Before you make the cut, it's important that the workpiece be fully supported—especially on long pieces that can tilt and cause an inaccurate cut or personal injury. Depending on the length of your workpiece, this may be as simple as extending the built-in sliding table extensions of your saw, as shown in the middle photo. For longer workpieces, consider one of the support techniques described on page 58.

A QUICK ACCURACY TEST

The majority of the saw cuts you'll make will be with the blade held at 90 degrees to the saw table. The quickest way to check that the blade is in fact exactly 90 degrees to the table is to make a quick accuracy test as described below.

Make a 90-degree cut. Start with a scrap piece of wood that has its top and bottom edges parallel and milled 90 degrees to each other. Butt the scrap vertically against your saw's fence and clamp it in place. Then make a 90-degree cut as shown.

Flip and check for a gap. Now take the cutoff and flip it over so its bottom edge is on top, and butt the two ends together as shown. Any gap (like the one shown here) indicates that the blade is not 90 degrees to the table and needs to be adjusted (see page 127 for instructions on how to do this).

Use a hold-down

One of the most reliable ways to ensure an accurate cut is to clamp your workpiece in place before making a cut. Even a quality crosscut blade will have a tendency to pull the workpiece slightly as it cuts into the wood, resulting in an inaccurate cut. Use either a built-in hold-down clamp (as shown in the top photo) or a shop clamp to securely lock the workpiece against the saw table or fence before making the cut.

Check your dust collection

It's also a good idea to make sure your dust collection device (or system) is hooked up properly and ready to do its job. For built-in dust bags (like the one shown in the middle photo), disconnect the bag and check to see whether it needs emptying. Do so if necessary and then reconnect it to your saw. For saws that are hooked up to shop vacuums or dust collectors, turn on the vacuum or collector and make sure air is being pulled freely into the dust chute.

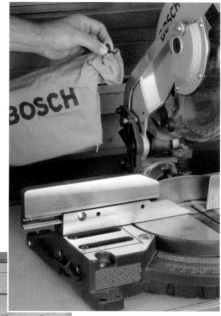

Wear appropriate protection

Finally, don appropriate protection, as shown in the bottom photo. For most miter saw work this means safety glasses to protect your eyes, hearing protection for your ears, and a dust mask to keep sawdust out of your lungs. Miter saws can and will throw small cut-offs, chips, and dust off at high speeds—even when hooked up to a dust collection system. They also tend to be quite loud, especially when the electric brake kicks in. Get into the habit now of protecting your eyes, ears, and lungs.

Setting Up for 90-Degree Cuts

In many shops, most of the cuts using the miter saw will be 90 degree cuts, where the blade is 90 degrees to the table and perpendicular to the fence. How accurate your cuts end up will depend on a properly tuned saw and correct technique. Use the quick accuracy test described on page 45 to make sure your saw is adjusted properly before cutting into your project parts. See chapter 6 for alignment procedures if the accuracy test fails. As to technique, much depends on how accurately the workpiece is positioned with respect to the blade. Positioning can be done freehand as described below, or with stops as described on pages 48–49.

Positioning with a cut mark

Positioning a workpiece freehand on the saw table with accuracy first requires that the workpiece be measured and marked with accuracy. The most common way to mark a workpiece is to make a single mark or short dash on the workpiece. Then the workpiece is slid over until the mark aligns with one edge of the saw blade, as shown in the photo at left. This can be difficult with standard compound saws that don't slide, as you have to sight down the blade, hoping that it will hit the mark. Even if you pull down on the main handle to lower the blade until it contacts the workpiece, odds are that the blade won't hit the mark—so a certain amount of guesswork is required. With a sliding compound saw, you can slide the saw carriage as needed to get the blade directly over the mark for alignment.

Positioning with a cut line

A better layout technique is to scribe a line across the full width of the workpiece with a pencil and a try or combination square. This line is easier to align to the blade as shown in the bottom left photo. That's because even if your saw doesn't slide, the blade will still contact the line when it is lowered for alignment. With a sliding compound saw, a line allows you to check alignment over the full travel of the blade.

Positioning with a laser guide

If your saw is equipped with a laser guide, either layout technique will work, as all you have to do is slide the workpiece over until the line to mark aligns with the laser (bottom right photo). Here again, the full-width line will allow you to check the alignment over the full width of the workpiece to get a better feel of how accurate the cut will be.

USING STOPS

We generally make freehand cuts only when accuracy isn't paramount. When precision is required, we reach for a stop to position the workpiece. In addition to adding accuracy by preventing the workpiece from moving during a cut, a stop also makes it super easy to make repeat cuts with precision. Stops can be positioned on the workpiece side or on the waste side, as described below and on the opposite page.

WORKPIECE-SIDE STOP

By far the most common way to install a stop is on the workpiece side of the saw fence. Positioning the stop on this side defines the length of the workpiece—you measure between the stop and the edge of the saw blade to set the length of the workpiece. Stops can be commercial, built-in, or shop-made.

Commercial and built-in stops. The stops that are built into many miter saws have limited use, as they typically can only extend out as far as the table extensions. For better range, consider one of the many fence and stop systems available as an accessory. These can extend out well past the saw table to define a greater range of workpiece length. The stop shown in the top photo fits onto a saw fence by Woodhaven (www.woodhaven.com) that attaches to a wide variety of saws (see pages 142–143 for step-by-step directions on how to install a commercial fence system).

Clamp on stop. At one time or another, most miter saw owners have made do with a scrap block stop clamped to their fence, as shown in the top right photo. This works fairly well for short workpieces, but unless you've added a longer auxiliary fence to your existing fence, this technique is fairly limited. Also, if

the clamp you're using doesn't lock the stop solidly in place, you can end up with inaccurate cuts. If you do use this type of stock, take the time to cut a small miter on the bottom inside edge (as shown) to serve as sawdust relief. This will prevent sawdust from building up between the stop and the workpiece (which can lead to inaccurate cuts as well).

Shop-made stop. If you're looking for an inexpensive stop system that offers more range than clamping a scrap to your miter saw fence, consider building the shop-made fence and stop system shown in the bottom photo and described in detail on pages 110–115. The unique stop in this system is also designed to extend back out over onto the miter saw table to handle shorter workpieces.

WASTE-SIDE STOP

Occasionally, you'll need to set up a stop on the waste side of the blade. This is typically reserved for cutting short or small workpieces to length. If you attached the stop to the workpiece side of the fence, your fingers would end up way too close to the blade. It's important to note that any stop you use on the waste side of the blade must be of the flip-up variety, as shown here. If you don't use a flip-up stop, the workpiece will get trapped between the blade and the stop, resulting in a dangerous situation where the cutoff will get thrown out at a high speed.

Commercial flip-up. Many of the commercial stops that are available come with a built-in flip-up feature, like the one shown in the bottom left photo and manufactured by Woodhaven (www.woodhaven.com). The stop is used by setting it the desired distance from

the blade. Then the workpiece is butted up against the stop and the stop is flipped up out of the way. When the cut is made, the waste piece (which is actually the workpiece) cannot be trapped against the blade.

Shop-made safe stop. Here's a shop-made version of the flip-up stop described above. It's just a scrap of MDF (medium-density fiberboard) that's cut in two. A small hinge connects the two pieces to provide the required flip-up action. In use, the stop is clamped to the table the desired distance from the blade, as shown in the upper right photo. Then the workpiece is butted up against the hinged portion and the hinged portion is flipped up out of the way, as shown in the lower right photo. Here again, this prevents the waste piece from being trapped between the stop and the blade.

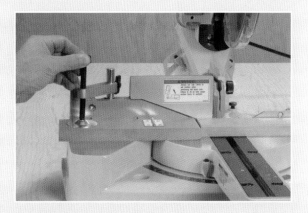

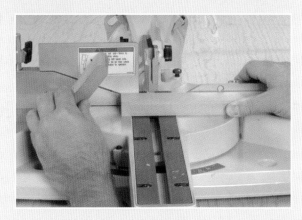

Crosscutting Techniques

Basic crosscutting technique is simple and straightforward. Position the workpiece and then make the cut. How you position the workpiece will depend on personal preference and often on the size of the workpiece. Depending on size, you may want to place the workpiece flat on the table or hold it vertically against the fence.

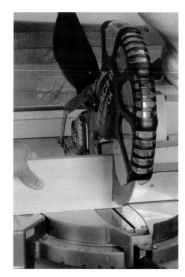

Horizontal crosscuts

You'll generally find that you'll get more accurate cuts when you place a workpiece flat on the saw table as shown in the top left photo. That's because this usually provides the most stable platform for the workpiece.

Vertical crosscuts

For shorter workpieces, some saw owners prefer to hold the workpiece vertically against the fence as shown in the top right photo. It's often more convenient to miter-cut molding (like baseboard) held this way than it is to lay it flat and angle the saw for a bevel cut.

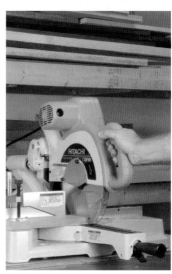

Crosscuts with a sliding compound saw

If you're making a crosscut on a sliding compound saw, you have two options for making the cut. Which one you use will depend on the size of the workpiece and personal preference. For narrow stock, you can lock the saw carriage in place and use the saw as if it were a chop saw and make the cut using either technique described above. For wider stock, you'll need to use the sliding feature of the saw. It's important to note that there is a very specific sequence to using a sliding compound saw—and it's the opposite of using a radial arm saw.

Here's how to make a cut. Start by pulling the carriage toward you until the blade is completely past the edge of the workpiece. Then lower the blade as shown in the lower left photo. Next, push the saw back to its starting position while keeping the blade down as shown in the lower right photo. Because of blade geometry, the teeth will push the workpiece firmly into the fence as it cuts, helping you achieve an accurate cut. On a radial arm saw, you pull the blade out into the workpiece—if you do this with a sliding compound miter saw, the blade will push the workpiece away from the fence—and could possibly shoot it into your midsection (ouch!).

Crosscutting Tips

In addition to how you position a workpiece (vertically or horizontally, as described on the opposite page), you can improve your cuts with any of the tips described on this page.

Preventing creep with sandpaper

One of the most prevalent problems associated with using a miter saw—"creep"—can be prevented in a

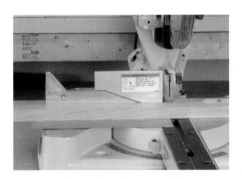

couple of ways. Creep is caused by the blade's tendency to pull or push a workpiece when it makes a cut. One way to reduce creep is to temporarily attach sandpaper to the saw table and/or fence as shown in the middle photo. The grit of the sandpaper "grabs" the workpiece and keeps it from shifting. Self-adhesive sandpaper works great for this, or you can attach standard sandpaper with rubber cement.

Preventing creep with a stop block

An even more reliable way to prevent creep is to use a stop block as shown in the middle right photo. This is particularly effective if you clamp the workpiece to the table with a hold-down, as shown here. A stop block by itself will keep a workpiece from being pushed away from the blade—but won't stop the blade from pulling the workpiece into the blade. For this you need either sandpaper (as described above) or a hold-down.

Reducing chip-out with kerf keepers

Although chip-out isn't an accuracy problem, it can damage your project parts. Chip-out occurs when a blade makes an unsupported cut. That is, there's insufficient support under the workpiece as the

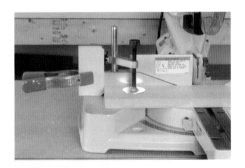

blade exits the bottom face of the workpiece. Without support (right scrap in bottom photo), wood fibers are torn from the surface. One way to prevent this is with the kerf plate or inserts. If your inserts are adjustable (middle left photo), adjust the inserts so they butt up against the blade. This will typically eliminate chip-out (left scrap in bottom photo).

Reducing chip-out with a zero-clearance table

If you don't have adjustable kerf inserts and instead have a kerf plate, you can install a zero-clearance table on top of your saw top. This is just a piece of $1/4$" hardboard that's fastened to your fixed table top with double-sided carpet tape (see page 43). This, too, will provide the needed support under a workpiece to prevent chip-out.

Miter Setup

Miter cuts are as simple to cut as straight crosscuts except that the saw blade is no longer perpendicular to the fence. The blade still must be 90 degrees to the table, so it's a good idea to first make a quick accuracy check as described on page 45 before cutting into your project parts.

Marking and layout

As with a straight crosscut, the first step to a precise cut is accurate measurement and layout. Although you can mark your workpiece with a single dash as you would for a straight crosscut, we recommend marking a full-width cut line as shown in the top photo. For 45-degree angles, a combination square works great for this. With other angles, you'll need to use a protractor or an adjustable-angle guide.

Setting the angle with detents

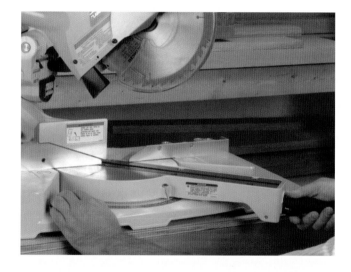

Once you've marked the cut line on your workpiece, you can adjust the saw blade to match that angle. If your cut angle matches one of the built-in detents, simply loosen the miter lock handle, lift up (or push down) the detent lock, and pivot the saw table until you reach the desired detent angle and release the lock to snap the saw table in position, as shown in the middle photo. Then re-tighten the miter lock handle.

Setting the angle with guides

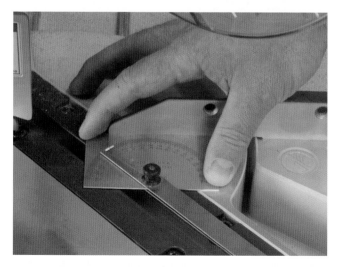

If the angle you're cutting doesn't match one of the built-in detents, you can either try to align the blade with the cut line you marked on the workpiece or use an adjustable-angle guide like the one shown in the bottom photo. Butt the head of the guide up against the saw fence, and pivot the saw table until the edge of the insert or kerf plate aligns with the blade of the guide as shown. Then lock the table in place by tightening the miter lock handle.

Using square stops

As soon as you angle the blade of a miter saw, the blade's tendency to grab and push or pull the workpiece increases dramatically, since the blade enters the workpiece at an angle. There are a number of ways to help prevent this, including adding sandpaper beneath the workpiece (as described on page 51) and using a hold-down. For the ultimate in accuracy, you'll also want to use a stop. There are two types of stops you can use with miter cuts: square and angled. If you want to use a square stop, you'll need to make sure that it's wider than your workpiece, as shown in the top photo. Otherwise, the angled portion of the workpiece will contact with the edge of the stop and the stop will not keep it from creeping when the cut is made.

Using angled stops

The ultimate stop for miter cuts is a stop that's angled to match the angled end of the workpiece, as shown in the middle photo. Make sure to orient the stop as shown so that it will capture the angled end against the saw fence.

Fine-tuning an angle

You'll often find that even with careful layout and positioning, you frequently will need to tweak the angle of a cut. If you're using a detent and your saw has a lockable detent override, engage it and re-adjust your miter angle. If your saw doesn't have a detent override, it's virtually impossible to tweak an angle at a detent location. One way around this is to shim the workpiece instead of trying to adjust the saw. A standard playing card works great for this. Just slip it between the workpiece and the fence, as shown in the bottom photo, to push the end of the workpiece out slightly and vary the cutting angle by just a hair. If this isn't enough, just add another card.

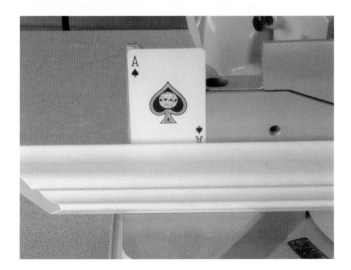

Miter Techniques

As with straight crosscuts, you have two positioning options for your workpiece: flat on the table, or held vertically against the fence. Similarly, which position you choose will depend on personal preference and the size of the workpiece. Narrow workpieces can be cut vertically, while wider pieces will need to be mitered lying flat on the table.

Compound saw with workpiece flat

The more stable of the two workpiece positions for mitering is laying the workpiece flat on the table, as this provides the best support. Once you've selected the angle, secure the workpiece with a stop and/or hold-down and make the cut by bringing the blade down into the workpiece (top left photo).

Compound saw with workpiece on edge

Holding the workpiece vertically on edge is commonly used when mitering trim. Trim carpenters find it faster and more convenient to angle the saw to the fence instead of tilting the blade to make a bevel cut (top right photo). As long as you hold the workpiece firmly against the fence (securing it with clamps works best), you end up with a fairly accurate cut.

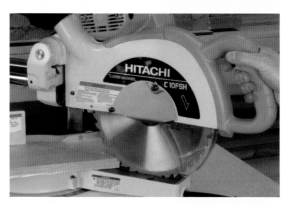

Mitering with a sliding compound saw

Mitering with a sliding compound offers two cutting options that depend on the width of the workpiece. For narrow stock, you can lock the carriage in place and make the cut as you would with a chop miter saw holding the workpiece in either position as described above. For wider work, you'll want to use the sliding feature. Here again, start by pulling the blade out past the edge of the workpiece and then lowering the blade, as shown in the middle photo. Then push the blade into the workpiece to make the cut, as shown in the bottom photo.

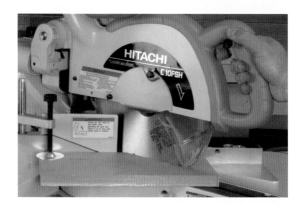

SNEAKING UP ON MITERS

Miter cuts are notorious for being a pain to cut. There are a couple of reasons for this. We've already mentioned that this type of cut tends to really push or pull the workpiece. Aligning the blade with the cut line is also a common problem.

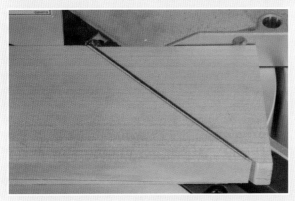 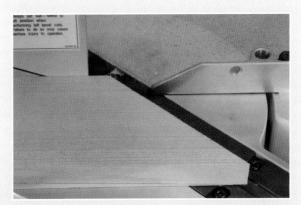

Sneaking up on a miter. One way to get around the problem of aligning a blade to a cut line is to make your first cut "fat" as shown in the top left photo; that is, make the cut on the waste side of the cut line so you can still see the line. Then slide the workpiece over just a hair closer to the blade and make another cut. Continue like this until you've snuck up on the cut line, as shown in the top right photo.

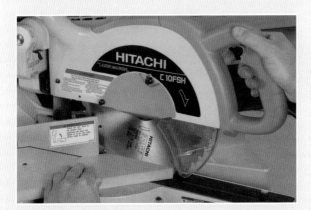 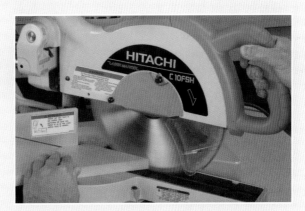

Trimming off a hair. Here's a nifty way to trim just a hair of a mitered piece. Start by lowering the saw blade until it's in its lowest position. Then butt the mitered end of the workpiece firmly up against the blade as shown in the bottom left photo. Now simply raise the blade, turn on the saw, and bring the blade back down to make the cut as shown in the bottom right photo. When you butt the workpiece up against the blade, the blade will deflect just slightly away from the workpiece. When you raise it, the blade will flex back to its normal position and will end up just slightly closer to the workpiece—enough to trim off just a hair. If this isn't enough, simply repeat this procedure as needed.

Cutting Wide Stock

Regardless of whether you've got a compound or a sliding compound miter saw, odds are that you'll occasionally need to cut stock that's wider than your saw can handle. There are a couple of techniques you can use for this. Under no circumstances will you be able to cut stock that's more than twice the stand width capacity of your saw. The double-pass method (described below) is used for stock up to twice your saw's normal width-cutting capacity. It's important to note that although this technique will allow you to cut wider boards, it generally does not create a perfectly straight cut edge. The table-shim technique (as described on the opposite page) is used for workpieces that are just slightly wider than your saw's standard width capacity.

Double-pass step 1

To use the double-pass method to cut wider stock, start by positioning your workpiece so the cut line is aligned with the edge of the blade. Then turn on the saw and lower the blade fully into the workpiece as shown in the top photo. This is in effect a plunge cut, so lower the blade gently into the workpiece. As soon as the cut bottoms out, raise the blade and turn off the saw.

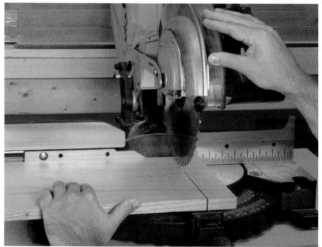

Double-pass step 2

Now flip the workpiece over so the cut edge is away from the fence. With the power off, lower the blade and slide the workpiece over until the blade fits into the kerf you just cut, as shown in the middle photo. This is the easiest way to align the two cuts.

Double-pass step 3

Raise the blade and turn on the power. Lower the blade into the workpiece to complete the second cut and sever the workpiece, as shown in the bottom photo. If you were careful with your alignment, the edge should be fairly straight and clean.

Table-shim method

When you need to cut a workpiece that's just slightly wider than your saw's standard capacity, use a table shim. This is nothing more than a scrap of plywood or MDF (medium-density fiberboard) that's cut to roughly the same width as your workpiece and is inserted underneath the workpiece, as shown in the top photo. What this does is raise up the workpiece so that it will be exposed to a wider portion of the saw blade, as illustrated in the middle drawing. Obviously, inserting a shim under the workpiece will decrease the thickness-cutting capacity of the saw—but it will allow you to cut a wider workpiece.

How thick the table shim needs to be depends on how wide a workpiece you need to cut. The thicker the shim, the thinner the workpiece you'll be able to cut. To determine the thickness of the shim, turn off power and lock the blade in its lowered position. Then measure out from the fence to the far edge of the blade the same distance as the width of the workpiece you need to cut. Mark this point and measure from it down to the saw table—this is how thick your table shim needs to be in order to cut fully through the workpiece.

Make the cut

Once you've determined how thick the table shim needs to be, slip it under your workpiece. Then align the cut line on the workpiece with the edge of the blade and lower the blade to make the cut, as shown in the bottom photo. A side benefit of this technique is that the table shim also serves as a zero-clearance table top and you'll end up with a virtually splinter-free cut.

CUTTING WIDE STOCK WITH A TABLE SHIM

Increased Width

Table Shim

Saw Table

Standard Width Capacity

Cutting Long Stock

Cutting long stock—often called "breaking down stock"—with a miter saw is one of the more common shop jobs. The problem with cutting long stock is that the saw tables on miter saws are inherently short to keep them portable. Without some form of outfeed support ,the stock is likely to tip up before, during, and after the cut. The problems this causes range from inaccurate cuts to potentially dangerous situations resulting in personal injury. Three common ways to support long stock are with support tables, outfeed rollers, and stands with built-in extensions.

Support tables

For miter saws that are in the shop—and mounted to a stand or cabinet—simple shop-made support tables (like the one shown in the top photo) do a terrific job of supporting long stock. These can be as simple as three scraps screwed together to match the height of the table and secured to the stand or cabinet. Alternatively, you can build a more deluxe table that has a built-in fence and stop system, like the one described on pages 110–115.

Outfeed rollers

The same outfeed roller that you use to support long cuts on a table saw, band saw, jointer, or planer can also be used to support long stock on the miter saw, as shown in the middle photo. Just raise the roller until it's level with the saw table and lock it in place. Since the roller is designed to roll, you'll need to use a hold-down to clamp the workpiece to the saw table to keep it from shifting during the cut.

Stands with built-in extensions

Finally, either a commercially made or shop-made stand that has built-in table extensions will do a good job of supporting most long stock. The shop-made stand shown in the bottom photo is described in detail on pages 92–105.

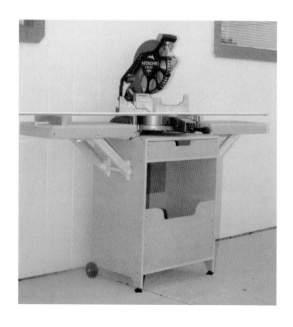

Cutting Thin Stock

Thin stock can be cut safely with a miter saw, as long as you use one of the safety measures described below. If you don't, the thin stock can vibrate and split during a cut, sending broken pieces and cutoffs away from the saw at high speeds.

Sandwich the stock between thick scraps

One of the safest ways to cut thin stock, particularly very thin stock like veneer, is to sandwich the thin stock between two thicker scraps as shown in the top photo. To keep the pieces of the sandwich tightly together, make sure to clamp the assembly to the saw table with a hold-down before making the cut.

Tape thin stock to thicker scrap

For stock that's slightly thicker, you can often get by with simply attaching the thin stock to a single thicker scrap with double-sided carpet tape, as shown in the middle photo. This will keep the thin stock from vibrating and splitting as well as serve to support the cut from below, resulting in a splinter-free cut.

Stack up thin stock and make gang cuts

When the stock is even thicker but there's still a possibility of vibration, consider stacking up multiple thin pieces (if possible) and making a gang cut, as shown in the bottom photo. This method works particularly well when making production runs of small parts.

Cutting Small Stock

The owner's manual of every miter saw we've read cautions about cutting small pieces. There are a couple of reasons for this. First, a small piece would require you to bring your hand way too close to the saw blade. Second, the small pieces tend to fly away from the saw when cut. There are, however, a couple of things you can do that will allow you to cut small pieces safely: Use a small-piece clamp and a zero-clearance fence.

Small-piece clamp

A small-piece clamp is basically an auxiliary holder that clamps to your saw table and lets you safely clamp and hold small pieces. The one shown in the top photo is just two scraps glued and screwed together to form a "mini-fence" for the saw. In use, the holder is clamped to the saw table with a hold-down and the small piece is either clamped to the holder or affixed with double-sided carpet tape. The advantage of using carpet tape is that it allows you to affix the waste piece as well to prevent flying pieces.

Zero-clearance fence

A zero-clearance fence is just a scrap of thin plywood or hardboard (at least $1/4$" thick) that's cut to match the height of your existing fence. The zero-clearance fence can be attached to your existing fence with double-sided carpet tape or, if it's thick enough, with screws driven in through the holes in your fence into the zero-clearance fence, as shown in the middle photo. Now when you make a cut, the cutoff or waste cannot be thrown backwards—the zero-clearance fence will prevent that.

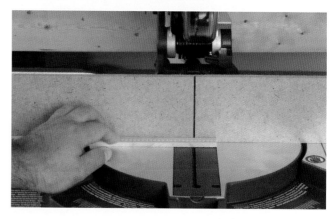

CHAMFERING WITH A MITER SAW

With a fine-tooth blade (60 teeth or more), you can use your miter saw to chamfer stock. Just set your saw for the desired angle—typically 45 degrees—position the workpiece for the desired chamfer width, and make the cut as shown in the bottom photo. Although it won't leave as clean a surface as a router, you may be surprised how smooth a chamfer that a sharp, clean, quality crosscut blade can produce.

Cutting Round Stock

Round stock can also be cut safely on the miter saw, as long as some provision is made to keep the stock from rotating during the cut. The three most common ways to keep the stock from rotating are to use a V-block, a beveled or coved molding strip, or a hold-down, as described below.

Use a V-block

A V-block is any scrap of wood into the surface of which you've cut intersecting miters. A V-block, like the one shown in the top photo, cradles the round stock and supports it during a cut. You'll still need to hold the stock in place in the V-groove, but the groove keeps the stock from rolling away. The quickest way to make a V-block is to fit a router with a V-groove bit and rout the groove in a scrap.

Use a beveled strip

You can also make a V-block quickly with a couple of strips of beveled or coved molding, as shown in the middle photo. Corner bead works well for this as long as the inside diameter closely matches the diameter of the round stock you're cutting.

Use a hold-down

Depending on the size of the round stock you need to cut and the hold-downs on your saw, you may be able to secure the workpiece with just your hold-down, as shown in the bottom photo. This generally works best on larger-diameter stock and with hold-downs that have a pivoting pad, like the hold-down shown here.

4 Advanced Miter Saw Techniques

Many of the basic cutting techniques for using a power miter saw are fairly intuitive. The advanced techniques are not. Compound cuts in particular often require mental gymnastics and numerous computations—especially when cutting crown molding—that can make your head spin. But not to worry, we'll show you some tricks that can make even this complex job simple. But there's more to crown molding than just cutting it—we'll also show how to install it, including tricks that trim carpenters use to ensure a professional-looking job.

We'll also take you through cutting and installing baseboard and window and door casing, along with specialty cuts like working with metal and plastic. All that you'll need to get the very most out of your miter saw.

Although the basic miter saw techniques will serve you well, it's the advanced miter saw techniques (like cutting crown molding) that will show you what you can really do with a miter saw.

Bevel Cuts

A bevel cut is any crosscut that's made with the blade perpendicular to the fence but tilted away from the vertical position. Most miter saws have positive stops at the 0-degree and 45-degree positions. A dual-tilting saw will stop at both 45-degree locations. All of the stops are usually adjustable; see page 129 for more on adjusting bevel stops. Some saws also have stops for cutting crown molding at 33.9 degrees (for 52/38-degree sprung molding). For more on cutting crown molding, see pages 68–73.

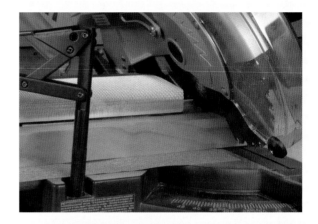

Adjust the fences as needed
Since you'll be tilting the saw blade away from 90 degrees, you'll likely need to move the sliding fence on the side of the saw that the blade is tilting toward. Most saws have a sliding fence that allows you to provide maximum support for 90-degree cuts and then slide the fence to the side to allow clearance for the saw blade and motor carriage, as shown in the middle photo. Adjust the fence as needed and make sure that it doesn't interfere with the cut by pulling the saw down into its cutting position.

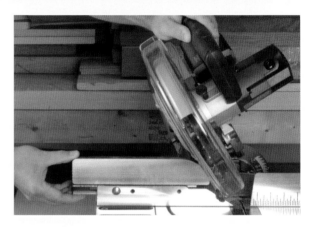

Using the scale to adjust the angle
Now you can adjust the saw to the desired bevel tilt. You can use the built-in bevel scale as shown in the photo at right, but these tend to be good only for rough positioning, as the marks of the scale are typically very close together. This makes it a real challenge to adjust to an angle like 43.2 degrees. You're better off using an angle guide (as described below) or a scrap reference block as described on page 65.

Using guides to adjust the angle
There are a number of adjustable-angle guides on the market that can be used to accurately adjust the tilt angle on your saw. The version shown in the far right bottom photo has a rectangular head that can rest on the table and an adjustable blade that's pivoted to the exact angle you want. Then it's just a matter of tilting the blade to match the angle of the angle guide.

Using a reference block to adjust the angle

The method we like to use to accurately adjust the blade tilt is to cut a reference block to the exact angle we need and use this to adjust the blade tilt, as shown in the top photo. Scribe the desired angle on a scrap block and adjust the miter angle (not bevel angle) on your saw to make the cut. Then use a protractor or angle guide to verify that it's the correct angle. If it isn't, tweak the angle and make another cut. Repeat until the block is the exact angle. To use the reference block, place it on the table and tilt the blade until it rests on the block as shown in the top photo.

Use a hold-down

A miter cut tends to pull or push a workpiece during a cut; a bevel cut tends to do this even more, as you're effectively cutting through thicker stock. When you bevel-cut through a 2×4 that's actually $1^{1}/_{2}$" thick, you're really cutting through 1.73"-thick stock. That's why it's so important to use a hold-down to keep the workpiece locked down solid against the saw table, as shown in the middle photo.

Preventing creep

You can also use a couple of other techniques to help prevent "creep"—the saw's natural tendency to shift a workpiece during a miter or bevel cut. One way to do this is to apply a piece of sandpaper to the saw top as shown in the bottom photo. The grit of the sandpaper will grip the workpiece and help keep it from shifting during a cut. Self-adhesive sandpaper works great for this, but you can also attach standard sandpaper with rubber cement. The other method to prevent creep is to use s stop block to lock the workpiece in position; see pages 48–49 for more on using stop blocks.

Compound Miter Cuts

A compound cut is any crosscut where the blade is set at an angle to both the saw table and the saw fence. In other words, the miter angle is not 90 degrees and the bevel angle is not 0 degrees. Because you're angling both the table and the blade, accurate compound cuts are challenging to set up. That's why it's important that you make a set of test cuts on scrap before committing to cut your project pieces— a certain amount of trial and error is usually required with most compound cuts. Even if you're using built-in stops or detents, you should make cuts in scrap first and verify that the angles are correct.

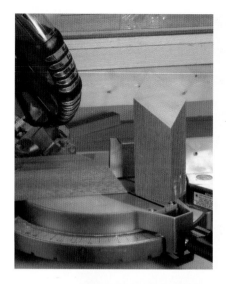

Marking and layout
Whenever we need to make a compound cut, we start by laying out both angles on a scrap of wood as shown in the middle photo. Here again, an adjustable-angle guide works great for this, but you can also use a protractor. Carefully lay out both angles so that they intersect.

Set the miter
Instead of setting both angles at once, we tend to set one angle first—the miter angle, as shown in the photo at right. Once it's set to the desired angle, we'll make a test cut on scrap and measure the cut to verify that it's correct.

Set the bevel
Then we'll adjust the blade tilt to the desired angle, as shown in the bottom photo. As before, we'll make a test cut on scrap and measure the bevel angle before cutting the first scrap on which we laid out the compound angle—it's just a lot easier tackling the angles one at a time.

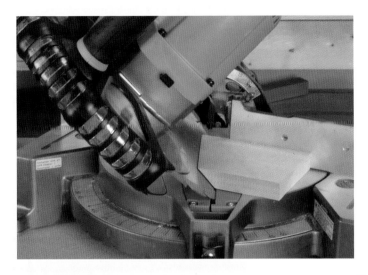

Adjusting the angle with a reference block

As with separate miter and bevel cuts, one of the most reliable ways to adjust a compound cut is to use a reference block. Scribe the desired angles on a scrap block and adjust the miter angle and bevel angles on your saw to make the cut. Then use a protractor or angle guide to verify that both are the correct angle. If they aren't, tweak the angles and make another cut. Repeat until the block is cut to the exact angles you want. To use the reference block, position it on the table and tilt the blade until its angle matches the angle of the reference block.

Use a hold-down

You know by now that a miter cut tends to push or pull a workpiece during a cut and that with a bevel cut this tendency increases. So it makes sense that if you make a miter and bevel cut at the same time, this shifting or "creep" is compounded. Any time you go to make a compound cut, be sure to use a hold-down to lock the workpiece in place and prevent creep, as shown in the middle photo. You can also use sandpaper on the table top and a stop to help keep the workpiece from moving.

Make the cut

You also know that cutting a workpiece at an angle means you're technically cutting a wider board, and that cutting a workpiece at a bevel means you're cutting a thicker board. So... when you make a compound cut, you're cutting into a wider, thicker workpiece. It just makes sense then to slow down the feed rate of the blade as it passes into and through the workpiece. If you cut too fast, odds are that the blade will deflect slightly, resulting in an inaccurate cut.

Cutting Crown Molding

Crown molding can dress up any room, adding a graceful touch with its classic profiles. Crown molding comes in a wide variety of profiles, as illustrated in the drawing below, and comes in various materials. You can find crown milled from solid wood—either hardwood or softwood—but this is becoming increasingly scarce. More commonly, you'll find crown molding made from medium-density fiberboard (MDF) or foam. Most MDF molding is sold pre-primed, making it easier to paint. You can also find some varieties with thin applied laminate or foil to give it the appearance of solid wood. The newer extruded foam varieties are much easier to install than conventional wood crown because they're lighter and cut very easily.

Typical sizes

As a general rule, you should choose crown molding that's around 3" to 4" wide for a standard 8' ceiling. Anything wider will appear out of scale. Also note that crown molding comes in varying lengths up to 16' and is sold by the foot. If you can't find molding that's long enough to span a room from corner to corner, you'll have to join the pieces together with a scarf joint. A scarf joint is made by cutting opposing 45-degree miters on the ends of the molding. The miter ends overlap to form an almost invisible joint.

Spring angle

The angle at which crown molding fits up against the wall and ceiling can also be specified. The two most common variations are 52/38-degree spring angle and 45/45-degree spring angle. For more on determining spring angle, see the sidebar on the opposite page.

Cutting and attaching crown

Although attaching crown molding to walls is fairly straightforward (see pages 74–77), cutting the complex molding to wrap around the corners of a room—especially in places that aren't 90-degree corners—can be tricky. Fortunately, with the aid of a power miter saw, this can be done without too much head scratching. There are three basic methods for cutting crown molding: with the molding flat on the table (see pages 69–70), with the molding angled against the fence (see pages 71–72), and with the aid of a jig (see page 73).

COMMON CROWN PROFILES

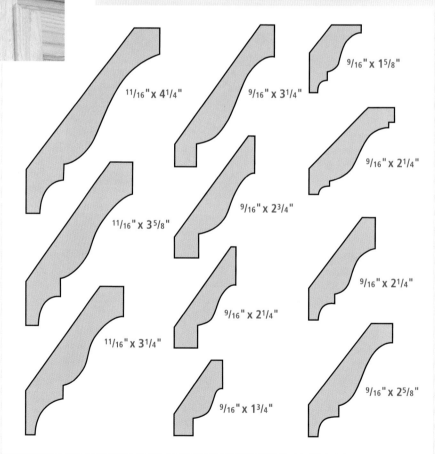

11/16" x 4 1/4"

9/16" x 3 1/4"

9/16" x 1 5/8"

11/16" x 3 5/8"

9/16" x 2 3/4"

9/16" x 2 1/4"

11/16" x 3 1/4"

9/16" x 2 1/4"

9/16" x 2 1/4"

9/16" x 1 3/4"

9/16" x 2 5/8"

MOLDING FLAT ON TABLE

If you recall from the section on making miter cuts in chapter 3, we indicated that you can usually get your most accurate cut with the workpiece lying flat on the saw table, as this provides the most stable foundation for a cut. This is also true for cutting crown molding. The molding we're cutting here is 52/38-degree spring molding. For 45/45-degree molding, see the chart on page 70 for the correct

miter and bevel angle settings. If you don't know your spring angle, see the sidebar below. Also, these settings assume your walls and ceilings are exactly 90 degrees to each other. If they're not, see page 78 for one way to measure this angle, and the chart on page 72 to determine the appropriate saw settings.

Set bevel to 33.9 degrees

To cut crown molding lying flat on the table, begin by setting the bevel angle to the desired angle (in our case here, 33.9 degrees). Some saws (like the Bosch saw shown in the middle left photo) have a built-in detent that makes setting this angle a snap.

Set angle to 31.6 degrees

Now you can angle the table to the desired angle (in our case, 31.6 degrees). As we described in chapter 3, it's best to make a test cut here if your saw table doesn't have built-in detent for this angle. Even if it does, it's a good idea to make a test cut and check the angle with a protractor or angle guide before proceeding.

DETERMINING SPRING ANGLE

The spring angle of a piece of crown molding is the angle between the back of the molding and the bottom flat surface that butts up against the wall. The two common spring angles for crown molding are: 52/38 degrees and 45/45 degrees. It's extremely important that you know the spring angle of the molding you intend to cut and install, as this angle will determine how you set your table angle and bevel tilt. If you don't know the spring angle of your molding, use an adjustable angle guide as shown in the photo above to measure it. Make sure to butt the guide up against the bottom flat of the molding. The molding in the drawing at right has a 52/38-degree spring angle.

BASIC CROWN ANATOMY

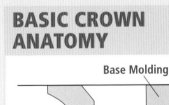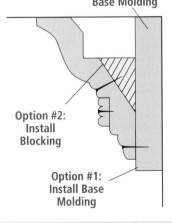

Base Molding

Option #2: Install Blocking

Option #1: Install Base Molding

Clamp the workpiece

As with any compound cut, you want to make sure that the workpiece is firmly clamped to the saw table to prevent it from shifting during the cut, resulting in an inaccurate angle (or angles). The hold-downs on most saws will work fine for this, as shown in the top photo. If the end of the clamp is not padded, consider slipping a strip of cork or rubber between the clamp end and the workpiece to prevent the clamp from dinging or denting the curved surfaces of the crown molding.

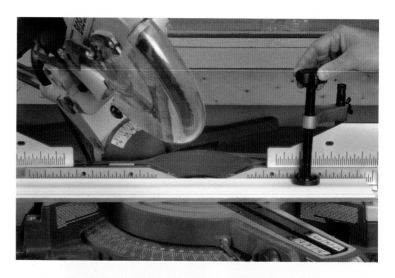

Make the cut

With the saw angles set and the crown molding firmly clamped to the saw table, go ahead and make the cut as shown in the middle photo. You'll want to use a slow feed rate here to prevent the tilted blade from deflecting as it cuts through the crown molding.

FLAT CROWN SETTINGS

The settings in the chart below are based on 90-degree walls. If your walls aren't 90 degrees to each other, see page 78 for a way to measure the angle, and the chart on page 72 for the appropriate saw settings.

	38° Spring		45° Spring	
Inside corner	Miter angle	Bevel angle	Miter angle	Bevel angle
Use the left end of cut.	31.6° right	33.9° left	35.3° right	30.0° left
Use the right end of cut.	31.6° left	33.9° right	35.3° left	30.0° right
Outside corner	Miter angle	Bevel angle	Miter angle	Bevel angle
Use the left end of cut.	31.6° left	33.9° right	35.3° left	30.0° right
Use the right end of cut.	31.6° right	33.9° left	35.3° right	30.0° left

MOLDING ANGLED ON TABLE

There's no doubt about it: Even with a tuned miter saw and a lot of patience, cutting crown can still be tricky. Much of this has to do with the fact that most walls and ceilings aren't 90 degrees to each other, and so you'll have to tweak the angles to make the crown fit well. It's a good idea to practice your first few cuts on scrap until you get the hang of it. It's also best to cut each piece a bit "fat" so you have some room to tweak the angles if necessary. The spring angle on the molding shown here is 45 degrees; if you're cutting 38-degree crown, see the chart on page 72 for the appropriate settings.

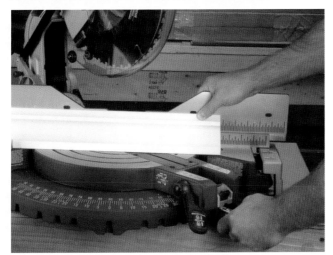

Position workpiece with crown stop

The standard phrase for cutting crown molding is "upside down and backwards." That is, when you position the workpiece on the miter saw, you want to turn the molding upside down and flip it end for end as shown in the top photo. If your saw has a crown stop (like the Bosch saw shown here), adjust the stop to hold the molding at the correct angle. Just slide the stop in or out until the top flat rests flush with the fence and the bottom flat sits flush on the saw table. If you don't have crown stops on your saw, you'll need to either clamp a strip across the saw table to hold the crown in place or use a crown molding jig like the one shown on page 73 or the shop-made version described on pages 86–91.

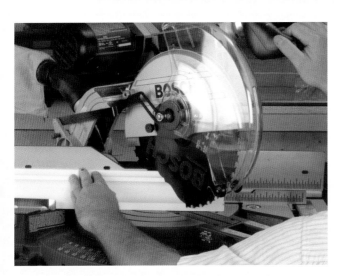

Set the miter to 45 degrees

Once the crown molding is angled correctly to the fence, all you have to do with 45/45 spring molding is adjust the miter table to 45 degrees, as shown in the middle photo, and lock it in place.

Make the cut

Now you can make the cut. Make sure to hold the molding in place with one hand to keep it from shifting during the cut, as shown in the bottom photo. Once cut, test the fit of the molding and tweak the angle if needed to get a good fit.

COMMON CROWN ANGLES AND SAW SETTINGS

Angle between Walls	52/38° Molding		45/45° Molding	
70°	41.3°	40.2°	45.2°	35.6°
71°	40.8°	39.9°	44.7°	35.2°
72°	40.3°	39.6°	44.2°	34.9°
73°	39.7°	39.3°	43.7°	34.6°
74°	39.2°	39.0°	43.1°	34.3°
75°	38.7°	38.6°	42.6°	34.1°
76°	38.2°	38.3°	42.1°	33.8°
77°	37.7°	38.0°	41.6°	33.6°
78°	37.2°	37.7°	41.1°	33.3°
79°	36.7°	37.4°	40.6°	33.0°
80°	36.2°	37.1°	40.1°	32.8°
81°	35.8°	36.8°	39.6°	32.5°
82°	35.3°	36.5°	39.1°	32.2°
83°	34.8°	36.1°	38.6°	32.0°
84°	34.3°	35.8°	38.1°	31.7°
85°	33.9°	35.5°	37.6°	31.4°
86°	33.4°	35.2°	37.1°	31.1°
87°	32.9°	34.8°	36.6°	30.8°
88°	32.5°	34.5°	36.2°	30.5°
89°	32.0°	34.2°	35.7°	30.2°
90°	31.6°	33.8°	35.2°	30.0°
91°	31.1°	33.5°	34.8°	29.7°
92°	30.7°	33.1°	34.4°	29.4°
93°	30.3°	32.8°	33.8°	29.1°
94°	29.8°	32.5°	33.4°	28.8°
95°	29.4°	32.1°	32.9°	28.5°
96°	29.0°	31.8°	32.4°	28.2°
97°	28.5°	31.4°	32.0°	27.9°
98°	28.1°	31.1°	31.5°	27.6°
99°	27.7°	30.7°	31.3°	27.3°
100°	27.3°	30.4°	30.6°	27.0°
101°	26.9°	30.0°	30.2°	26.7°
102°	26.5°	29.7°	29.8°	26.4°
103°	26.0°	29.3°	29.3°	26.1°
104°	25.6°	29.0°	28.9°	25.8°
105°	25.2°	28.6°	28.4°	25.5°
106°	24.8°	28.3°	28.0°	25.1°
107°	24.5°	27.9°	27.6°	24.8°
108°	24.1°	27.6°	27.1°	24.5°
109°	23.7°	27.2°	26.7°	24.2°
110°	23.3°	26.8°	26.3°	23.9°

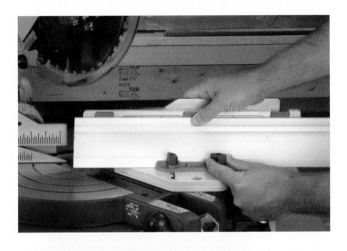

USING A CROWN MOLDING JIG

If you want to cut crown molding with the molding angled up against your fence, and your saw doesn't have built-in stops to hold the molding in place, consider using a crown molding jig. Crown molding jigs do one thing and they do it well—hold your workpiece at the correct angle for the cut. The crown molding jig we're using here is manufactured by Bench Dog Tools (www.benchdog.com). Alternatively, you can make your own jig; see pages 86–91 for more on this.

Position the workpiece in the jig

To use a crown molding jig, start by placing your workpiece in the jig as shown in the top photo. On most jigs there's an adjustable bar that you can slide back and forth to position the molding so that the top flat is flush with the fence of the jig and the bottom flat of the molding sits flush on the base of the jig. Once it's positioned properly, lock the sliding bar in place with the threaded knobs provided.

Position the jig on the saw

With the molding held at the correct angle, all you have to do now is adjust the saw for the desired angle (45 degrees in our case) and slide the jig over until your layout mark aligns with the saw blade, as shown in the middle photo. It's a good idea to lock the jig in place by clamping it to the saw fence before making your cut.

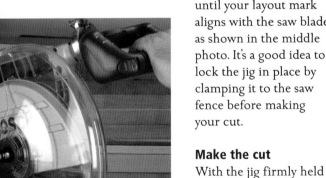

Make the cut

With the jig firmly held or clamped in place, go ahead and make the cut. As always, it's best to make the cut a bit "fat" in case you need to tweak the angle and re-cut to get a good fit.

Installing Crown Molding

Because crown molding rests against a wall and ceiling at an angle, it has only two small flat sections that make contact. This makes it difficult to attach, especially on walls and ceilings, since you need to hit a stud or joist for the nail to hold. To get around this problem, most trim carpenters use one of three methods to create a solid nailing base: mitered nailing blocks, plywood blocking, or a flat base molding (see below). To install any of these, you'll first need to locate the wall studs using an electronic stud finder and then mark these locations with a pencil.

Mitered nailing blocks

The simplest way to provide better support to your crown molding is to cut a set of mitered nailing blocks and attach these to the wall studs as shown in the top photo. To make these, just measure the flat portion of the molding and miter-cut scraps of 2×4 to create an identical flat on the long side of the block. Attach these at the marked wall studs, and you'll find it's much easier to install and attach the molding to the nailing blocks than it is to attach the molding directly to the wall studs.

Plywood blocking

To create even better support for your crown molding, consider ripping angled strips of plywood to fit behind the molding. In most cases, two beveled pieces of plywood stacked on top of each other will provide a very stable nailing base. Attach the plywood blocking to the wall studs at each marked location as shown in the bottom left photo. Now you can attach the crown molding to the plywood blocking anywhere along its length. This is particularly useful when you need to join together short pieces of mold-ing with scrap joints—there will always be something to nail into with plywood blocking.

Flat base molding

Another way to provide continuous nailing support is to first attach a flat molding to the wall as shown in the bottom right photo. Flat molding is easy to attach to the wall at the stud locations and provides a continuous nailing surface for the crown molding. In addition to providing a nailing surface, these moldings can also provide a more complex and pleasing profile, especially if you shape the bottom edge with a router before installing the molding.

TYPICAL INSTALLATION SEQUENCE

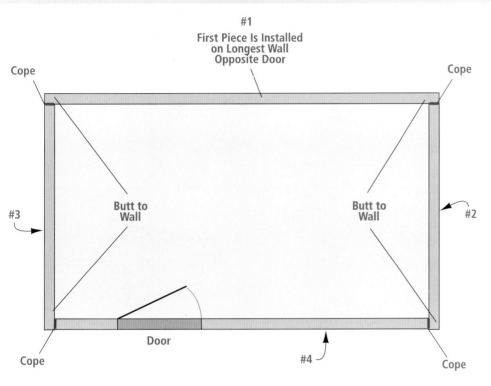

#1
First Piece Is Installed
on Longest Wall
Opposite Door

Cope

Cope

Cope

Cope

#3

#2

Butt to Wall

Butt to Wall

Door

#4

Installation sequence

If you're planning on coping the corner joints (see pages 78–79), there's a recommended sequence for installing the molding. This sequence (as illustrated in the top drawing) is designed to offer the best possible appearance of the molding.

Butt first piece

Start by installing molding on the longest wall opposite the doorway leading into the room. Butt the ends of the molding into each corner as shown in the middle photo. Then cope the joint to fit against this molding and continue working your way around the room, as illustrated in the drawing. The easiest way to attach crown molding is with an air-powered finish nailer (you can find these at most rental centers). A finish nailer will drive and set the nail exactly where you want it with the pull of a trigger. Sure, you can attach crown with a hammer and nails, but the chances of dinging the molding are extremely high. Also, since the finish nailer is used one-handed, your other hand is free to hold the molding—not so with a hammer and nails.

Cope the second

With the first strip of molding in place, expose the miter on the end of the next piece and use a coping saw to remove the waste as described on pages 78–79. Test the fit of the coped end against the molding that's butted into the corner as shown in the bottom photo, and fine-tune the coped end as needed for a good fit (see page 79).

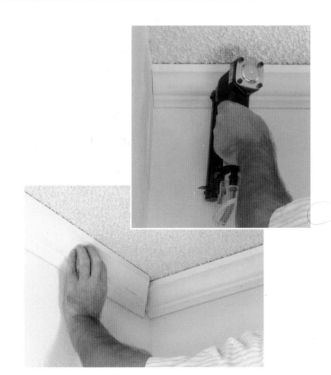

Secure at studs/blocking

Once you've obtained a good fit between the strips of molding, you can secure the molding. Start by securing the molding at the studs, mitered angle blocks, plywood blocking, or flat base molding, as shown in the top photo. If you're securing the molding directly to the studs, try to wiggle the molding after each nail is driven in to make sure you hit the stud. Drive in another nail if it's loose.

Secure at ceiling joists

If the ceiling joist in the wall that you're working on runs perpendicular to the wall, you can also secure the crown molding to these joists. Start by locating them with an electronic stud finder, and mark each location. Then drive in a nail at each location to firmly attach the molding, as shown in the middle photo.

Pin the miters at corners

If you have to wrap around an outside corner (as shown in the bottom right photo), it's a good idea to pin together the corners by driving a nail or two into the top edges of the molding as shown. This will do two things. It'll help pull the miter joint closed and will also create a stronger molding. Note that if you're using an air nailer, don't pinch the molding together with your fingers and then drive in a nail. If you do, there's a real good chance you'll drive a nail into your finger.

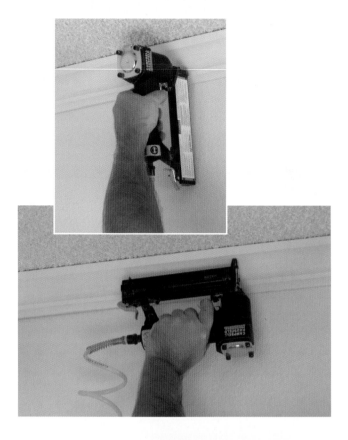

BURNISHING OUTSIDE CORNERS

If you notice small gaps when you miter together an outside corner, you can close the gaps with an old carpenter's trick called "burnishing." All you have to do is press the shank of a screwdriver firmly over the miter joint as shown in the photo above. This will crush the wood fibers to fill in any gaps.

USING A DIGITAL PROTRACTOR

If you put up a lot of molding, consider purchasing a digital protractor like the Bosch DWM 40L shown in the top right photo. A digital protractor takes all the guesswork and computations out of installing molding. That's right—all you have to do is measure the wall angle with the protractor, and it will compute the miter and bevel angle settings for your saw; see below. Then just set up your saw with the angles provided by the protractor and make your cut to get a perfect fit. What could be easier than that?

Measure the angle. To use a digital protractor, open up the legs of the protractor and butt each leg flat against the wall surfaces and read the digital display.

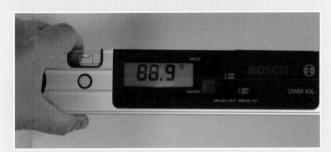

Store the wall angle. If your protractor has a store or hold function, press the hold button to store the wall angle so that you can compute the miter saw settings.

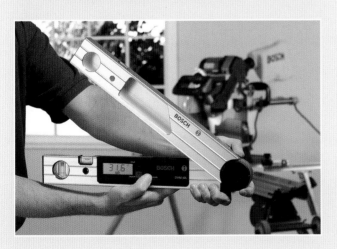

Compute the settings. For the Bosch protractor shown here, press the BV/MT button and the display will show the value of the miter setting. The miter setting is displayed along with the "MTR" indicator. Make a note of this setting or just adjust your saw miter to this angle. Then press the BV/MT button again to show the bevel angle. The bevel setting will appear along with the "BVL" indicator. Make a note of this setting or just adjust your blade tilt to this angle. Your saw is now set up to cut the molding for a perfect fit.

Coping Crown Molding

Coped joints are used extensively by savvy trim carpenters and woodworkers who want moldings to intersect at inside corners without the gaps normally associated with miter joints. There are two halves to a coped joint, as illustrated in the top drawing. On one half, the molding profile is left intact and simply butted into the corner of a wall or cabinet. The second half is the part that's coped to fit the profile of the molding butted into the corner.

When done properly, a coped part will butt cleanly up against the molding profile with no gaps. Not only will this joint fit nicely when completed, but it will also stay that way: There's less exposed end grain than on a miter joint, which will expand and contract as the seasons change. Miter joints are notorious for opening and closing as the humidity changes, producing a varying-width gap throughout the year.

Expose the miter

To make a coped joint, start by installing one molding piece so that it butts into the corner. The next step is to expose the cope on the molding to be coped. This can be done easily on the miter saw, as shown in the middle photo and illustrated in the bottom drawing. The idea here is to cut the end as if you were doing an inside miter. The miter cut will expose the wood that needs to be removed to fit against the matching profile of the first piece.

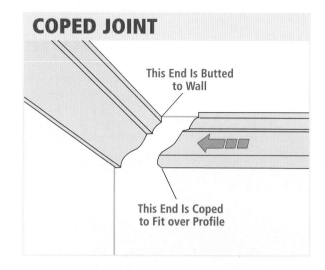

COPED JOINT

This End Is Butted to Wall

This End Is Coped to Fit over Profile

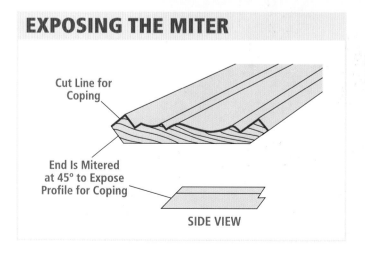

EXPOSING THE MITER

Cut Line for Coping

End Is Mitered at 45° to Expose Profile for Coping

SIDE VIEW

Define the profile

Once you've exposed the cope, you can remove the waste. Before you do this, it's a good idea to highlight and define the profile that you'll be cutting. Just run the tip of a pencil along the profile as shown in the top photo. This dark line will be a lot easier to follow than just the profile. This is particularly helpful when cutting solid-wood molding, where the face and edge of the exposed miter are the same color.

Cut with coping saw

A coping saw gets its name from coping a joint, as shown in the middle photo. The blade of the saw is held in a tensioned frame that is adjustable. Most

coping saws accept a $6^5/_8$"-long, very thin, narrow blade with fine teeth—typically 15 to 32 teeth per inch. The blade on a coping saw can be pivoted to make it easier to follow a curve. Before you cut into the waste portion of the molding, it's a good idea to make a series of relief cuts first where the molding profile changes direction. Then go back and cut out the waste, taking care not to cut into the face of the molding. What you're after here is a 45-degree cut in the opposite direction of the exposed miter. Beveling the cut in the opposite direction will allow the profile to fit over the molding butted up against the wall.

Fine-tune with file

After you've removed the exposed waste, try fitting the coped piece against a scrap of the molding. Note any areas where there are gaps, and mark these with a pencil. If there are large gaps, go back to the coping saw and remove the bulk of the waste. If the gaps are small, you can fine-tune the coped profile to fit better. A small round or half-round file will generally make quick work of this, as shown in the bottom photo. Be sure to angle the file back toward the back of the molding to keep from filing into the exposed profile. Alternatively, a dowel or screwdriver wrapped with sandpaper can quickly remove waste from curved areas. Test the fit frequently and continue fine-tuning until the coped part fits perfectly against the molding profile.

Working with Baseboard

Baseboard is one of simplest moldings to cut and install because it sits flat against a wall. There are two ways to cut baseboard: flat against the table or vertically against the fence (see below). See the chart below for common settings for each technique (note that these settings assume 90-degree walls).

Inside and outside corners

Since baseboard typically wraps around the perimeter of a room, odds are that you'll encounter both inside and outside corners, as illustrated in the drawing at right. Outside corners can be mitered, and inside corners are best coped (see pages 78–79) to get the best possible fit.

Flat on the table

Since you usually get your most accurate cut with a workpiece lying flat on the saw table (as this provides the most stable foundation for a cut), you'll get your most accurate cut with baseboard lying flat on the saw table, as shown in the left middle photo.

Vertical against the fence

Many trim carpenters prefer cutting baseboard held vertically, as shown in the right middle photo, because it's faster and easier to angle the miter angle than the bevel angle. Which method you use will depend on your personal preference.

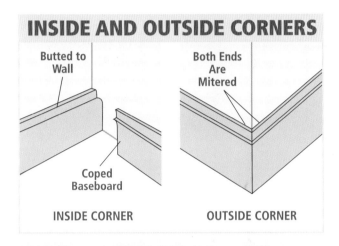

INSIDE AND OUTSIDE CORNERS

Butted to Wall

Coped Baseboard

INSIDE CORNER

Both Ends Are Mitered

OUTSIDE CORNER

SETTINGS FOR CUTTING BASEBOARD

Piece Being Cut		Vertical Molding		Horizontal Molding	
		To left of corner	To right of corner	To left of corner	To right of corner
Inside corner	Miter angle	Left at 45°	Right at 45°	0°	0°
	Bevel angle	0°	0°	45° left	45° right
	Molding position on saw	Bottom against table	Bottom against table	Top against fence	Top against fence
	Finished side	Keep left side of cut	Keep right side of cut	Keep left side of cut	Keep right side of cut
Outside corner	Miter angle	Right at 45°	Left at 45°	0°	0°
	Bevel angle	0°	0°	45° right	45° left
	Molding position on saw	Bottom against table	Bottom against table	Top against fence	Top against fence
	Finished side	Keep left side of cut	Keep right side of cut	Keep left side of cut	Keep right side of cut

Installing Door and Window Casing

Door and window casing is easy to install. If your door or window jambs are 90 degrees to each other, it's a snap. Otherwise, you'll need to sneak up on a perfect fit by tweaking the angles as needed. To

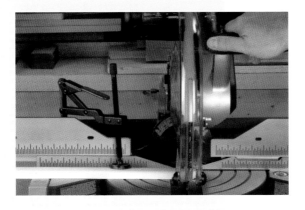

install door or window casing, start by marking the reveal on each jamb. A reveal is a slight offset between the trim and the jamb. It allows for easier installation and provides a shadow line for visual interest. The easiest way to mark this is to set the blade of a combination square so it protrudes $1/8$". Then place a pencil against the blade of the square, press the head of the square against the jamb, and run these around the perimeter to mark the reveal.

Miter-cut the casing to length

Now you can measure the length of your casing and cut the pieces to length. We prefer to cut the miter first on an over-long piece, as shown in the top photo. Then cut the casing to length as shown in the photo above left. We've found that it's easier to sneak up on a perfect fit this way.

Attach to studs

Once you've got the casing cut to length, position each piece one at a time so the inside edge is flush with the marked reveal line. Nail the trim to the jamb and studs with finish nails spaced about 12" apart, as shown in the photo at left.

Lock-nail the joints

To close any gaps at the miter joints and strengthen the joint, "lock-nail" the joints together as shown in the bottom photo. Here again, use a finish nail and make sure to stay away from the front edge or else you'll split the trim piece.

Cutting Metal

You can cut metal on a miter saw so long as it's non-ferrous. This means no steel or iron. Aluminum is the safest metal to cut, as long as you use a metal-cutting blade like that shown in the top photo. The LU90M blade by Freud (www.freudtools.com) is designed specifically to cut thin, non-ferrous metal extrusions such as aluminum storm window frames without damaging the delicate profiles. The high number of carbide tips and the slightly positive hook angle allow these blades to slice quickly and cleanly through the material without binding.

Position work correctly

Because aluminum is soft and easily deformed, it's important that you either position the workpiece correctly on the saw table or make sure to support it with a scrap of wood, as illustrated in the drawing at right.

Make the cut

Since you're cutting through metal, it's a good idea to use a fairly slow feed rate as you pass the blade into the workpiece (bottom left photo). Caution: Be sure to wear eye protection when cutting metal. All it takes is a single aluminum shaving in the eye to end up with a trip to the emergency room.

Clean up!

The metal shavings that can damage your eye can also cause a lot of damage to your saw—in particular, if they work their way down into the table pivot mechanism. If they do, they can scratch the sliding surfaces and you'll notice a grinding feeling as you pivot the saw table. If this happens, stop and take your saw into a service center to have the shavings removed and the surfaces smoothed. If you're mechanically inclined, you can do this yourself; see pages 140–141 for more on this. The moral of this story is to make sure to thoroughly vacuum up any metal shavings as soon as you're done with each cut, as shown in the bottom right photo.

POSITION WORK CORRECTLY

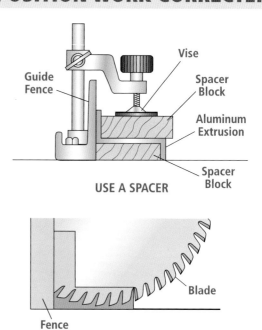

USE A SPACER

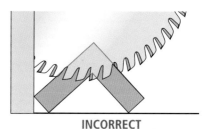

Cut through Thinnest Section
CORRECT

INCORRECT

Cutting Plastics

Plastics can also be cut safely on the miter saw. Although you can use a standard crosscut blade on most plastics, you'll find it better to use a special plastic-cutting blade, like the Freud LU94M series shown in the top photo. You can cleanly cut acrylic, polycarbonate, vinyl, and most other plastics without melting with this blade. By combining numerous carbide tips with a specially modified triple chip grind and a negative hook angle, these blades will give the clean, smooth cut that you would expect from the high tooth count but produce less heat, keeping the cut edges crisper.

Zero-clearance table

The shavings generated from cutting plastic can also foul up the inner workings of your saw. They also tend to really clog up the gap in your kerf table between the kerf inserts. That's why we recommend adding a zero-clearance table underneath the workpiece, as shown in the middle photo. This is just a strip of $1/4$" hardboard or plywood that's cut to roughly the same width as your workpiece.

Make the cut

As with any other miter saw cut, it's best to lock the workpiece in place by clamping it to the saw table with a hold-down. The feed rate you choose will depend on the type of plastic you're cutting. Opaque plastics like the UHMW (ultra high molecular weight) plastic we're cutting in the bottom photo can tolerate a fairly fast feed rate. Transparent plastics (like Lexan) are best cut with a slower rate. Take care not to go too slow or you'll end up melting the plastic instead of cutting it cleanly.

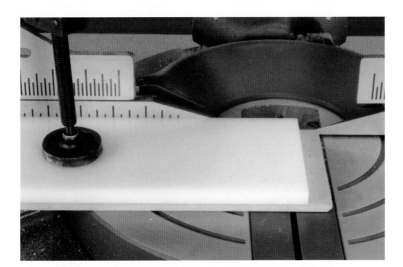

5 Miter Saw Jigs and Fixtures

Since miter saws are pretty much ready to go right out of the box, they don't require a lot of jigs and fixtures. There are, however, a couple of jigs and fixtures that you can build that will allow you do to more with your saw—and do it safer. This chapter features five jigs and fixtures ranging in complexity from very simple to complex. Simple jigs include a wide-angle jig for cutting angles greater than 45 degrees, and an auxiliary table with clamps that attach to your saw and let you securely clamp a workpiece in place for a cut. Slightly more complex jigs are an adjustable crown molding jig that holds molding in perfect position for accurate cuts, and a fence/table system with an adjustable stop for making precision repeat cuts. The most involved project is a miter saw stand complete with built-in storage and extension wings to support long cuts; these wings also collapse for storage and transport.

Four of the five jigs featured in this chapter are shown here: a miter saw stand with lift-up extension wings, an auxiliary table with clamps, a wide-angle jig, and a fence system with an adjustable stop.

Adjustable Crown Molding Jig

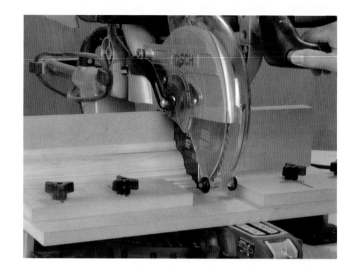

Crown molding has a well-deserved reputation for being tough to cut. One of the main problems with cutting crown when it's held angled to the saw fence is keeping it at the correct angle—and holding it there solidly while you make the cut. Both of these problems are solved with the adjustable crown molding jig shown in the top photo and illustrated in the exploded view on the opposite page. The jig features a solid double-layer back fence that attaches to your fence and a pair of adjustable cleats that allow you to accurately position crown molding in a variety of sizes and spring angles (for more on crown cutting technique, see pages 68–73).

Attach fence to base

To build the adjustable crown molding jig, start by cutting the parts to size per the materials list on the opposite page. Assembly begins by first attaching the fence to the base with glue and screws, as shown in the middle photo. If you're using MDF (medium-density fiberboard), as shown here, you'll want to make sure to drill pilot holes for the screws both in the bottom face of the fence and in the edge of the base before screwing the parts together. If you don't, odds are the MFD will split when you drive in the screws.

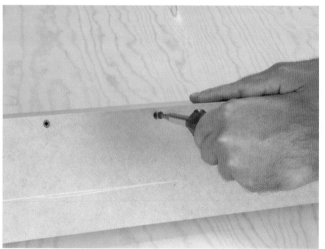

Attach support fence

Because we wanted the fence to be extra stable and not flex when crown molding was pressed against it, we added a support fence to the face of the fence as shown in the bottom photo. After gluing and clamping the support fence to the fence, further secure it by driving screws up through the base and into the bottom edge of the support fence, as illustrated in the detail drawing on the bottom of page 88.

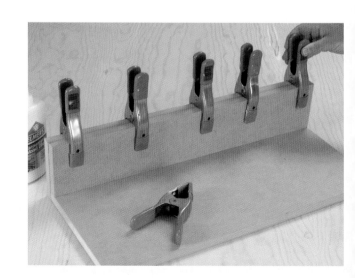

EXPLODED VIEW

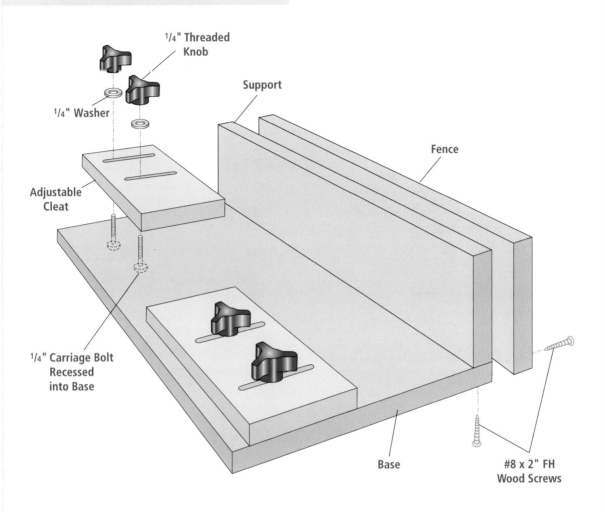

¼" Threaded Knob

Support

Fence

¼" Washer

Adjustable Cleat

¼" Carriage Bolt Recessed into Base

Base

#8 x 2" FH Wood Screws

MATERIALS LIST

Part	Quantity	Dimensions
Base	1	10" × 24" – ¾" MDF
Fence	1	5" × 24" – ¾" MDF
Support	1	4¼" × 24" – ¾" MDF
Adjustable cleats	2	3¾" × 10" – ¾" MDF
Carriage bolts	4	¼" × 1½"
Washers	4	¼"
Threaded knobs	4	¼" threads

Rout slots in cleats

With the base assembled, you can turn your
attention to the adjustable cleats. The cleats
are slotted to accept carriage bolts that pass
up through the base and cleats; they're held
in place with threaded knobs, as illustrated
in the drawing below. The slots are 1" and
6" in from the outside edge of each cleat
and $1/2$" in from each side (they're $2^3/4$" long
and $1/4$" wide). To make these slots, start by
marking the start and stop of each slot and
then drill a $1/4$" hole through the cleat at
each hole location. We found it easiest to remove
the waste between the slot holes with a router fitted
with a $1/4$" straight bit mounted in a router table, as
shown in the top photo. Alternatively, you could use
a coping saw to cut out the waste.

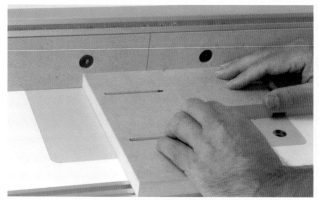

Locate mounting hardware: step 1

Now you can use the slotted cleats to locate the
holes in the base for the mounting hardware. To do
this, place one cleat on each back corner of the table
as shown in the middle photo. Adjust each cleat so
its back and side edges align with the back and side
of the base.

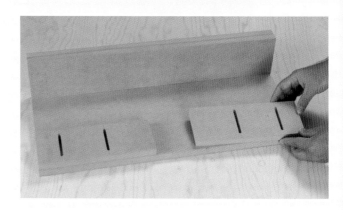

CROSS SECTION OF CLEAT/BASE

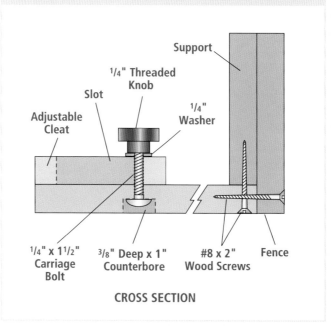

Support

$1/4$" Threaded
Knob

Slot

$1/4$"
Washer

Adjustable
Cleat

$1/4$" x $1^1/2$"
Carriage
Bolt

$3/8$" Deep x 1"
Counterbore

#8 x 2"
Wood Screws

Fence

CROSS SECTION

Locate the mounting hardware: step 2

The simplest way to accurately locate the mounting hardware that passes up through the slots in the cleats is to use a brad-point bit. Just insert a 1/4" brad-point bit at the end of each slot and tap the end of the bit with a hammer, as shown in the top photo. The pointed tip of the bit will make an indentation exactly at the center of the slot. Repeat this for both ends of all the slots; then set aside the adjustable cleats.

Drill the counterbore

To transfer these hole locations to the underside of the base (where you'll be drilling the counterbores for the carriage bolts), simply fit your smallest drill bit in your drill (typically 1/16") and drill through the base at each location. Then flip the assembled base upside down and drill 1/4"-deep, 1"-diameter counterbores at each hole location, as shown in the middle photo. These counterbores recess the carriage bolts below the underside of the base so the base will sit flat on the table of your miter saw.

Drill the shank holes

With all the counterbores drilled, insert a 1/4" bit in your drill and drill the shank holes for each carriage bolt as shown in the bottom photo. This is a snap, as the bit you used to drill the counterbore left a perfectly centered indentation in the bottom of each counterbore that you can use to start the 1/4" bit.

Install carriage bolts

At this point you can install the four carriage bolts. Insert one in each counterbore and drive it with a hammer as shown in the top photo. Make sure to drive it in until it bottoms out in the counterbore—if the face of your hammer won't fit into the counterbore, use another carriage bolt or stove bolt as a pin punch to drive it in. Not only will this ensure that the bolt doesn't protrude out of the bottom of the base, but it also "locks" the carriage bolt in place. This is due to the square portion of the shank directly under the head—the old "square peg in a round hole" concept actually works here.

Add the cleats

All that's left is to add the cleats to the base. Just slip each cleat over its appropriate carriage bolts. Then slip on washers and threaded knobs (middle photo). Check the motion of each adjustable cleat to make sure they slide smoothly back and forth. If they don't, remove them and widen the slots slightly as needed with a file or sandpaper.

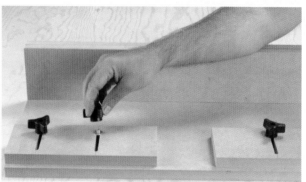

AN ALTERNATE STOP

The adjustable crown molding jig is designed to hold crown angled up against the fence. Because of this, the molding needs to be cut "upside down and backwards"—a technique that trim carpenters have used for a long time. This can get confusing when it's time to cut the molding. One way around this is to build a pair of alternate stops, as illustrated in the drawing at right. The stops hold the molding as it will be installed on the wall—no mental gymnastics required. The alternate stops are just modified adjustable cleats; just add the vertical support and sliding stop. In use, molding is placed with its back edge against the saw fence. Then adjust the sliding stop and adjustable cleat to hold the front edge of the molding at the correct angle—then make the cut.

ALTERNATE STOP

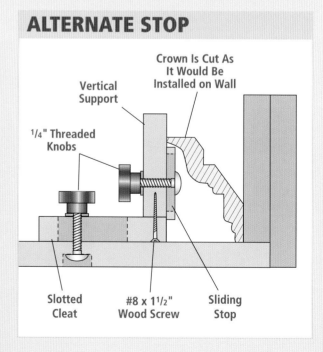

Vertical Support

Crown Is Cut As It Would Be Installed on Wall

1/4" Threaded Knobs

Slotted Cleat

#8 x 1 1/2" Wood Screw

Sliding Stop

USING THE JIG

The adjustable crown molding jig is simple to use, but you'll first need to attach it to your saw and set it up to cut as described below. The cleats adjust in and out to provide a wide range of motion for holding a variety of moldings, as illustrated in the drawing below.

RANGE OF CROWN CROSS SECTION

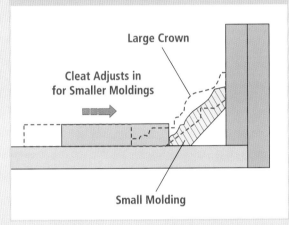

Large Crown

Cleat Adjusts in for Smaller Moldings

Small Molding

Attach the jig to your saw. Position the crown molding jig on your saw table so it's centered from side to side and butted up against the saw fence. Then mark hole locations through the saw fence onto the back of the fence. Drill pilot holes and secure the jig to the saw with #8 × 1¼" wood screws.

Reset the cutting depth. To prevent your blade from cutting through the base of the jig, reset your saw cut depth to cut about ¼" into the base (top photo). If your saw doesn't have this feature, you can usually slip a shim between the saw arm and the stop that limits the depth of cut.

Adjust the cleats. Now place the molding against the fence and slide the adjustable cleats forward until the molding is held at the correct angle; tighten the threaded knobs to secure the cleats to the jig.

Make the cut. Support the molding with one hand to keep it from shifting side-to-side as you make the cut, and then lower the blade into the molding using a steady feed rate until the cut is complete. Stop the saw and then raise the blade—this prevents the blade from deflecting on the upstroke and shaving too much off the freshly cut end.

Miter Saw Stand

Regardless of their size or type, all miter saws need a work surface to rest on. Trim carpenters sometimes clamp their saws to the lowered tailgate of their trucks at jobsites. But this isn't terribly convenient, so many folks spring for a commercial stand. These can easily cost hundreds of dollars. If you like the idea of a stand but don't want to spend the money, consider building the inexpensive shop-made miter stand shown here and illustrated in the exploded view on the opposite page. Our stand is loaded with features. It has a handy drawer for storing blades, wrenches, and manuals and a lower pull-out bin for storing cutoffs. A pair of lift-up extension arms lock into place to support long workpieces and then fold back down for transport. A pair of wheels and adjustable levelers at the bottom of the saw

make it easy to roll around and set up level on-site in minutes.

Cut grooves/rabbets in sides

Construction of the miter saw stand begins with the sides. Cut a pair of these to size per the materials list on the opposite page. Then cut a rabbet for the top shelf and a pair of grooves for the middle and bottom shelf as illustrated in bottom drawing. We cut these with a dado blade on the table saw, as shown in the bottom photo, but you could also cut them with a router fitted with a straight bit. All of these are $3/8$" deep and $3/4$" wide. The middle groove is $4\,3/4$" down from the top of the side, and the bottom groove is 3" up from the bottom of the side.

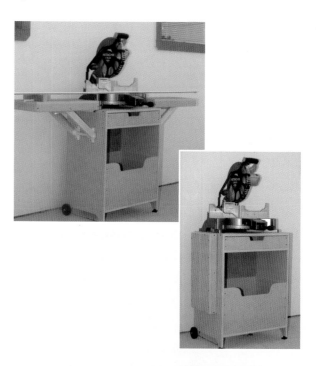

GROOVE/RABBET DETAIL

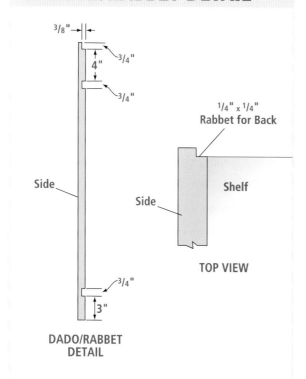

3/8"

3/4"

4"

3/4"

1/4" x 1/4"
Rabbet for Back

Side

Shelf

Side

TOP VIEW

3/4"

3"

DADO/RABBET
DETAIL

EXPLODED VIEW

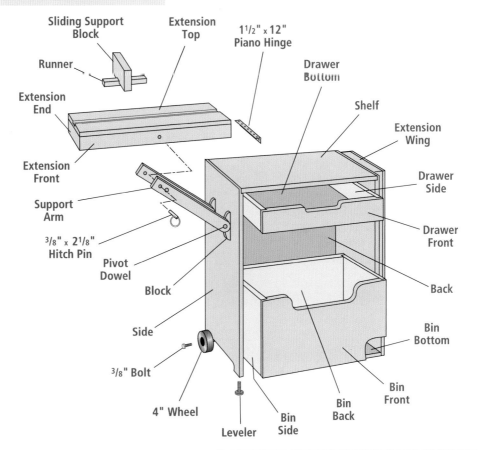

Sliding Support Block

Runner

Extension End

Extension Front

Support Arm

$3/8" \times 2^1/8"$ Hitch Pin

Pivot Dowel

Block

Side

$3/8"$ Bolt

4" Wheel

Leveler

Bin Side

Extension Top

$1^1/2" \times 12"$ Piano Hinge

Drawer Bottom

Shelf

Extension Wing

Drawer Side

Drawer Front

Back

Bin Bottom

Bin Front

Bin Back

MATERIALS LIST

Part	Quantity	Dimensions
Sides	2	$18" \times 34" - 3/4"$
Shelves	3	$17^3/4" \times 25^1/2" - 3/4"$
Back	1	$25^1/2" \times 31" - 1/4"$
Drawer front/back	2	$3^7/8" \times 24^5/8" - 3/4"$
Drawer sides	2	$3^7/8" \times 16^3/4" - 3/4"$
Drawer bottom	1	$16^5/8" \times 23^5/8" - 1/4"$
Bin front/back	2	$14" \times 24^5/8" - 3/4"$
Bin sides	2	$14" \times 16^3/4" - 3/4"$
Bin bottom	1	$16^5/8" \; 23^5/8" - 1/4"$
Extension top	2	$12" \times 24" - 3/4"$
Extension front/back	4	$2" \times 24" - 3/4"$
Extension ends	4	$2" \times 10^1/2" - 3/4"$
Runners	2	$3/4" \times 3/4" - 8"$

Part	Quantity	Dimensions
Sliding supports	2	$1^1/2" \times 1^3/4"$ * $- 10"$
Piano hinges	2	$1^1/2" \times 12"$
Support arms	4	$2" \times 16" - 3/4"$ hardwood
Dowels	4	1" diameter, 10" long
Pivot blocks	4	$2" \times 5" - 3/4"$
Hitch pins	4	$3/8" \times 2^1/8"$, cotterless
Wheels	2	4" diameter, $3/8"$ axle hole
Wheel axles	2	$3/8" \times 2^1/2"$ stove bolt
Wheel washers	4	$3/8"$
Wheel lock nuts	2	$3/8"$
Levelers	2	$1/4" \times 2^1/4"$ threaded knobs
Threaded inserts	2	$1/4"$

*Height of the sliding support will depend on the height of your saw table.

Rabbet the sides for the back

Next, cut a $1/4" \times 1/4"$ rabbet on the back inside edges of each side to accept the back that's added later. We also cut this with a dado blade on the table saw as shown in the top photo. Note that you'll need to bury the head of the dado blade in a scrap-wood auxiliary fence to make this cut safely.

Lay out the recess on sides

The bottom of each side is recessed to create pairs of legs: two for the rear wheels and two for the front levelers, as shown in the middle photo. Each recess starts 2" in from the sides and is 3" high. You can lay out the recess rectangular, or round over the inside corners as we did (we used a 3" radius).

Cut out the recess

Once you've got the recess laid out on one side, go ahead and cut it out with a saber saw (as shown in the bottom photo) or with a coping saw. When you're done, use this to mark the recess on the other side, then cut out that recess as well.

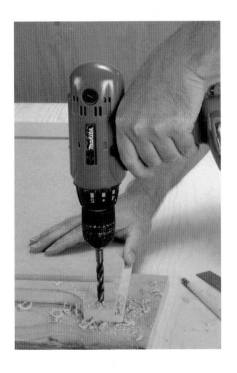

Locate and drill the axle holes

The holes for wheel axles are located 1" up from the side bottom and 1" in from the back edge (assuming you use a 4"-diameter wheel). Locate and mark a hole on each side. Then drill the appropriate-sized hole at each location for your axle—ours were $^3/_8$" stove bolts—as shown in the top photo.

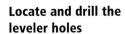

Locate and drill the leveler holes

Next you can drill holes in the front bottom edge of each side for the threaded inserts that accept the leg levelers, as shown in the middle photo. For levelers, we used $^1/_4$" × $2^1/_4$"-long threaded knobs, but you could also use stove bolts. It's just that the threaded knobs provide a more stable foundation. The holes for the levelers are 1" in from the front edge of each side and centered on the thickness of the side.

Assemble the sides and shelves

With the sides complete, cut the three shelves to size per the materials list on page 93. Then lay out and drill assembly holes through the sides, centered on the rabbet and grooves you cut earlier. Apply glue to one edge of the shelves and place them in their appropriate grooves and rabbet in one side. Make sure that the shelves are flush with the front of the sides—they should also be flush with the rabbet in the back edge of the sides. Now drill through your assembly holes into the shelves and drive in screws as shown in the bottom photo. We spaced our screws about every 4" starting 1" in from each edge. Apply glue to the other edges of the shelves and attach the remaining side using the same procedure you used for the first side. Check to make sure that the assembly is square, and set it aside for now. (It's best to attach the back later, after you've added the support arms.)

Cut the drawer and bin joinery

Cut the drawer and bin front/back and sides to size per the materials list on page 93. The front and back are joined to the sides with a simple rabbet joint (to align the parts) and glue and screws. Start by cutting $3/8$"-deep × $3/4$"-wide rabbets on the sides of the drawer and bin front/back as illustrated in the drawing below. We buried the head of a dado blade in an auxiliary fence and cut these on the table saw, as shown in the top photo. You'll also need to cut a $1/4$" × $1/4$" groove along the bottom edge of each part to accept the drawer and bin bottoms; these grooves are $1/2$" up from the bottom edges, as illustrated below.

Lay out the handle recesses

Instead of handles, we decided to keep the front of the stand clean by using handle recesses. Use the

handle recess illustration on the bottom of the opposite page as a guide to lay out a recess in the drawer front and bin front, as shown in the bottom photo. Here again, you could go with a rectangular recess or a rounded one as shown here.

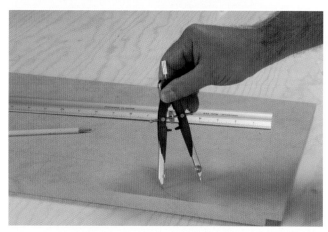

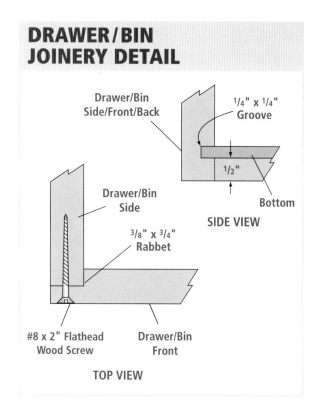

DRAWER/BIN JOINERY DETAIL

Drawer/Bin Side/Front/Back

$1/4$" x $1/4$" Groove

$1/2$"

Bottom

SIDE VIEW

Drawer/Bin Side

$3/8$" x $3/4$" Rabbet

#8 x 2" Flathead Wood Screw

Drawer/Bin Front

TOP VIEW

Cut out the handle recesses

After you've laid out the two handle recesses, go ahead and cut them out with a saber saw (as shown in the top photo) or a coping saw. When done, sand the corners smooth with a drum sander mounted in an electric drill or drill press, or a dowel wrapped with sandpaper. Then soften all the edges of the drawer and bin by giving them a quick once-over with a piece of sandpaper or a radius plane.

Assemble the drawer and bin

Before you can assemble the drawer and bin, you'll need to cut bottoms to size from $1/4$" hardboard. The most accurate way to do this is to dry-clamp the drawer and bin parts together and measure from groove to groove and subtract $1/8$" for clearance. Once you've cut the bottoms to fit, apply glue to the bottom grooves and to the rabbets in the front/back. Assemble the drawer and bin and drill pilot holes for screws; then drive in screws as shown in the middle photo. Set the completed drawer and bin aside for now.

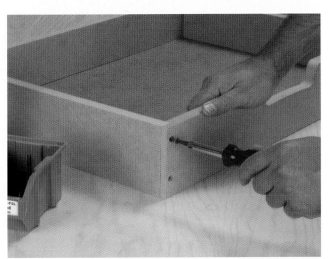

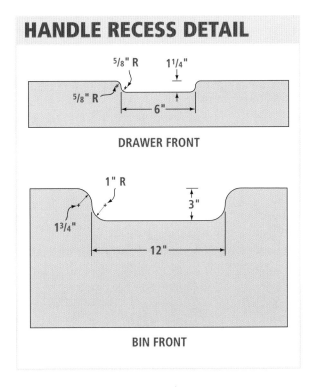

HANDLE RECESS DETAIL

DRAWER FRONT

$5/8$" R $1^1/4$"

$5/8$" R

6"

BIN FRONT

1" R

3"

$1^3/4$"

12"

Cut a groove in the extension tops

With the drawer and bin complete, the next step is to build the extension arms for the stand. Each extension consists of a top, front/back, and ends. Cut these to size per the materials list on page 93. The extension top is grooved to accept the runner of a sliding support block (see the exploded view on page 93). This block is cut to size once your miter saw is attached to the stand. One advantage of this system is that the stand is universal—all you have to do if you change miter saws is make a new sliding support block. Cut a 3/8"-deep, 3/4"-wide groove centered on the length of the top. We did this with a table saw fitted with a dado blade, as shown in the top photo. Cut a groove on both extension tops.

Assemble the extensions

Now you can assemble the extensions. Start by gluing and screwing the front and back to the top. Then slip the ends between the front/back and screw them to the top and front/back as shown in the middle photo. As always, if you're working with MDF, you'll want to drill pilot holes first before driving in the screws. Also, since you'll be chamfering the top in the next step, make sure to locate the screws toward the inside edges of the front/back and ends.

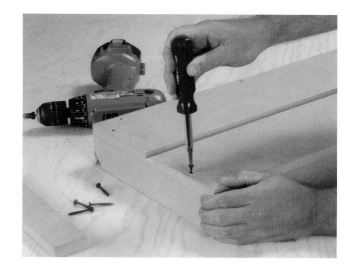

Chamfer the top edges

To complete the extension, run a router fitted with a chamfering bit around the top perimeter of both extension tops as shown in the bottom photo. This chamfer is both for appearance and to keep the sharp edges from dinging a workpiece if it comes in contact with the extension top (something that's inevitable when working with long stock).

Attach the extension hinges

The extensions attach to the sides of the stands via a pair of $1\frac{1}{2}" \times 12"$-long piano hinges. Don't substitute smaller hinges for these, as they won't provide the full-length support that a piano hinge offers. Start by attaching one hinge flap to the bottom edge of each extension end. The most accurate way to drill perfectly centered holes for the hinge screws is to use a self-centering bit (often referred to by the brand name Vix bit). These nifty bits sport an inner and outer sleeve that spin around a twist bit. When the tip of the self-centering bit is inserted in a hinge hole and depressed, an inner sleeve retracts up into the outer sleeve. This positions the twist bit so it can drill a perfectly centered hole for the hinge screw. Once you've drilled the holes, drive in the screws as shown in the top photo.

Locate the extensions on the sides

With one hinge flap attached to each extension, the next step is to locate the extensions on the sides of the stand. What you're looking for here is an extension that's centered from front to back on the side of the stand and the knuckle of the hinge is centered on the top edge of the side. Position each extension and then mark where it will rest on the sides, as shown in the middle photo. This will allow you to accurately locate the loose hinge flap when you attach it to the sides in the next step.

Attach the extensions to the stand

A helper is useful for this next step. Have your helper hold the extension in the extended position so that it aligns with the marks you made previously on the sides. Then, while holding the hinge level with the top edge of the stand side, drill pilot holes for the piano hinge screws. Drill the two extreme hole locations first and drive in the screws. Then drill the rest and secure the hinge to the side with the remaining screws, as shown in the bottom photo.

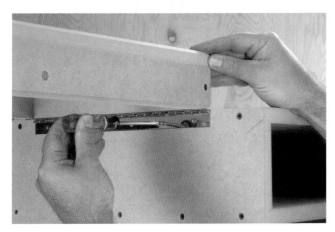

Drill holes in supports for the dowels

Once the extensions have been attached to the stand, you can make the supports and pivot blocks that hold the extensions in their upright positions. Each support consists of a pair of support arms spanned by dowels. The dowels pass through the pivot blocks, which are attached later to the sides of the stand. Cut four support arms and four dowels to size per the materials list on page 93. Then lay out and drill holes in the support arms for the dowels as shown in the top photo. Hole size and locations are illustrated in the drawing below.

Round over the support ends

To allow the ends of the support arms that butt up against the stand sides to pivot freely, one end of each arm must be rounded over, as illustrated in the detail drawing below. One way to do this is to lay out the radius and cut it to rough shape with a saber saw or coping saw. Then sand a smooth curve with a disk sander (as shown in the middle photo) or with a drum sander in the drill press. You can also file or sand a smooth radius by hand.

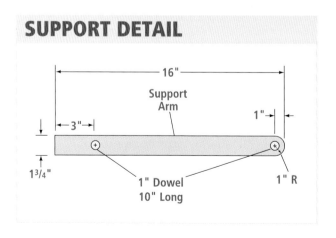

SUPPORT DETAIL

16"

Support Arm

3"

1"

1¾"

1" Dowel
10" Long

1" R

Drill holes in the pivot blocks

The first step to making the pivot blocks is to lay out and drill a hole in each one for the support arm dowel to pass through. It's easiest to do this while the block is still square. Lay out the hole location as illustrated in the drawing below, and drill a 1"-diameter hole in each pivot block as shown in the top photo.

Lay out the pivot blocks

Now you can lay out the shape of the pivot block as illustrated in the drawing below. The ends of the block slope away from the center hole to make it easier to attach the block to the side of the stand. Instead of duplicating this layout four times, consider cutting and smoothing one to shape and then using this as a template to mark the other three pivot blocks, as shown in the middle photo.

PIVOT BLOCK DETAIL

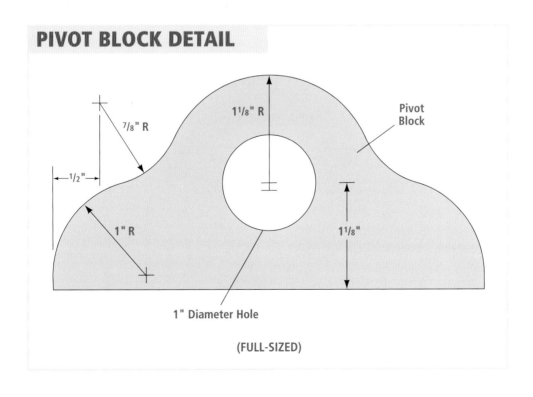

$7/8$" R

$1/2$"

$1^{1}/_{8}$" R

Pivot Block

1" R

$1^{1}/_{8}$"

1" Diameter Hole

(FULL-SIZED)

Cut the pivot blocks to shape

With all the pivot blocks laid out, you can cut them to shape. A band saw (like the one shown in the top photo) will make quick work of this, but you can also cut these to size with a saber saw or coping saw. To make it safer to cut these small blocks, consider laying them out on over-long blanks like the one shown here. This way you can use the extra length as a handle to keep your fingers away from a moving blade. This "handle" also provides a much-needed clamping surface if you're cutting these small blocks to size with a saber saw.

Sand for smooth pivoting action

After you've cut all the pivots blocks to shape, smooth the curves with a drum sander fitted in a drill press or electric drill, or with a dowel wrapped with sandpaper. Odds are that you'll also want to sand the interior of the dowel hole a little to create a smooth pivoting action. A dowel wrapped with sandpaper (as shown in the middle photo) works great for this. Just make sure to stop frequently to check the action—you don't want to remove too much wood and end up with a sloppy fit. At this time, you'll also want to drill a pair of mounting holes in each pivot block to attach them to the stand sides. These are located roughly 3/4" in from each end and centered on the thickness of the block.

Assemble the supports

Now that all of the support parts are machined, you can assemble the supports. Start by slipping a pair of pivot blocks onto one of the 10"-long dowels. Then push the ends of the dowels into the holes in one of the support arms. Position the other support arm over the exposed ends of the dowels and tap it in place as shown in the bottom photo.

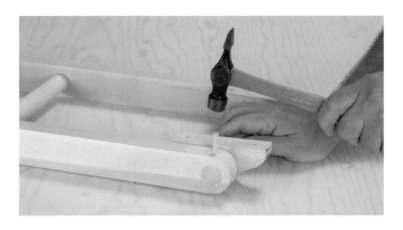

Lock the dowels in place

Since there could be significant weight on the extension and support arms, we didn't want to rely on glue alone to keep the dowels from pivoting in the support arms and working loose—they're supposed to pivot only in the pivot blocks. With this in mind, we drilled holes through the support arms and into the 1" dowels centered on each dowel. Then we drove in cross pins ($1/4$" dowels) into these holes to lock the dowels in place, as shown in the top photo.

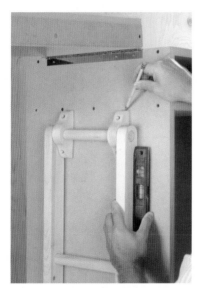

Locate the pivot blocks

With the supports complete, the next step is to locate them on the sides of the stand. Start by lifting an extension into its upright position. Then center the support from front to back on the side of the stand and position it so the tops of the pivot blocks are approximately $5^{1}/_{2}$" down from the top edge of the side and level. Use a level to also verify that the support arms are plumb, as shown in the middle photo, before marking the position of the pivot blocks on the sides as shown.

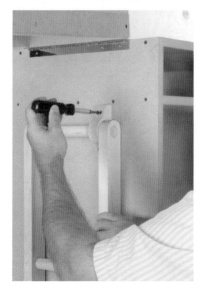

Attach the pivot blocks

With the pivot blocks in place, push an awl through each of the mounting holes you drilled previously in each block to mark the mounting hole locations. Then set the support aside and drill pilot holes in the sides at each location. Reposition the support and drive screws through the pivot blocks and into the sides as shown in the bottom photo. Repeat for the remaining support. Once the pivot blocks are in place, cut a back to fit the stand and attach it to the sides and shelves with glue and finish nails.

Level the extensions

Now that the supports are in place, you can position them to support the extensions. To do this, first raise the extension into its upright position and temporarily clamp the support to the inside edge of the extension. Use a level to make sure the extension is level before clamping the support in place as shown in the top photo. Clamp both sides of the support.

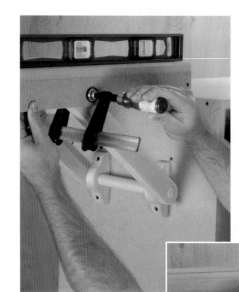

Drill holes for the hitch pins

Remove one of the clamps and drill a $3/8$"-diameter hole through the front or back of the extension and through the support arm. Make sure to locate these holes so that they pass through the support arms as centered as possible. Repeat this procedure for the remaining three support arms—you want hitch pin holes in each support arm to fully support the extension top.

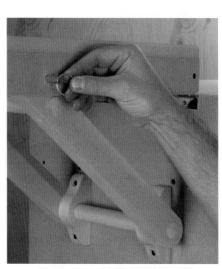

Insert the hitch pins

When you've drilled all the hitch pin holes, go ahead and lock the extensions in their upright positions by inserting the hitch pins through the extension holes and into the support arms as shown in the bottom photo. In the beginning these pins will be snug, but they'll loosen up a bit with wear, and it'll be easier to insert and remove them. You can also rub a little paraffin on the pins to help them slide in and out smoothly.

Determine the height of the sliding support

All that's left to complete the miter saw stand is to make the sliding supports. Each consists of a sliding block and a runner. The runner is just a scrap of 3/4"-sqaure hardwood cut to a length of 8". To determine the height of the sliding support, you'll first need to place your miter saw on the top of the stand (you can also drill holes in the top shelf and mount the saw now if you want).

Then place a 3' or 4' level on the saw table so it extends out over the extension as shown in the top photo. Measure from the bottom edge of the level to the top of the extension, and that's the height of the sliding support.

Cut a groove in bottom for the runner

After you've cut the sliding supports to size, cut a 3/8"-deep, 3/4"-wide groove centered on the length of the support. This groove will accept the runner and help to lock it in place. We cut this groove with a table saw fitted with a dado blade, as shown in the middle photo. You can also cut this with a router fitted with a straight bit or simply cut the groove with a chisel.

Attach the runner

Apply glue to the groove in the sliding support and insert the runner. Drill a pilot hole through the runner and into the support and drive in a screw to secure the runner as shown in the bottom photo. Place the runner in the groove in the extension top and make sure that it slides smoothly back and forth so you can position it wherever you need the support. If it binds, sand the sides of the runner slightly. Double-check that the top is level with your saw table by spanning your level from the sliding support to the saw table, and adjust the height of the sliding support as needed.

Miter Saw Table with Clamps

One of the best ways to ensure accurate cuts on the miter saw is to securely clamp the workpiece in place during the cut. That's because on many cuts—especially miters, bevels, and compound cuts—the blade has a tendency to pull or push the workpiece from side to side as it enters and cuts through the workpiece. Although many saws come with built-in hold-downs, some do not. And even on saws that do offer hold-downs, the hold-downs often don't work so well or they have a very limited range of clamping ability.

We designed a simple auxiliary table with clamps that solves both problems. Our table attaches to the saw's fence and features a movable clamp that fits on either side of the blade to clamp a wide variety of workpiece sizes. The clamp is a special version called a toggle clamp that snaps down or "toggles" to lock a workpiece in place. The toggle clamp attaches to a clamping block that is held in place on the table via a threaded stud, as shown in the top photo and illustrated in the exploded view on the opposite page. The threaded stud threads into T-nuts let into the underside of the base.

Lay out T-nut locations on base

To build the miter saw table with clamps, start by cutting the parts to size per the materials list on the opposite page. Since you'll be attaching T-nuts to the underside of the base, it's important to locate these so they're not in the path of the blade. To do this, draw a line down the center of the base and a pair of intersecting lines at 45 degrees (the red lines in the middle photo). Then lay out the locations of the inserts, making sure they are well away from these common cut lines. For the Bosch saw shown here, we located the T-nuts 6" in from sides and 3", 7", and 11" in from the front edge of the base. Note that if you miter-cut at different angles, make sure to check first to be sure the blade won't hit one of the T-nuts. Centerpunch each of the hole locations.

Drill counterbores for the T-nuts

Once you've located the positions of the T-nuts, fit your drill or drill press with a 1" Forstner bit and drill a $1/8$"-deep counterbore at each location, as shown in the bottom photo, so the T-nuts will sit well below the surface of the base.

Drill barrel holes for the T-nuts

Now you can drill the shank holes for the barrels of the T-nuts. The size of these holes will depend on the diameter of the barrels on your T-nuts. Choose a bit that's just slightly larger than the barrel diameter, and drill holes centered in the counterbores through the base as shown in the top photo. Make sure to slip a scrap under the base to keep from drilling into your work surface.

EXPLODED VIEW

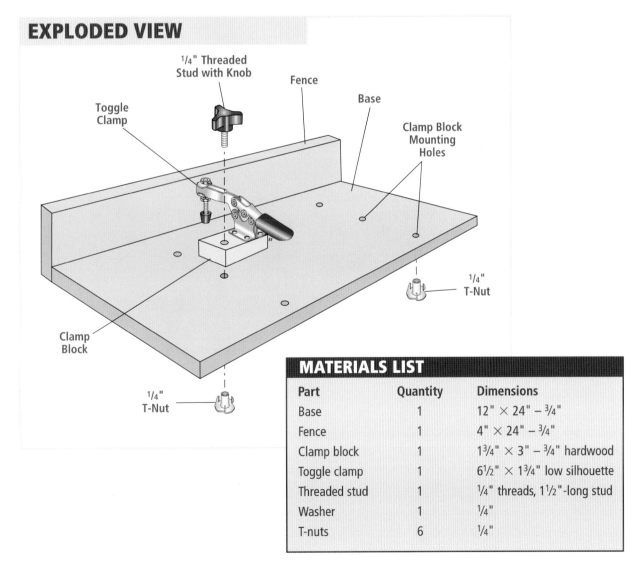

1/4" Threaded Stud with Knob

Fence

Base

Toggle Clamp

Clamp Block Mounting Holes

1/4" T-Nut

Clamp Block

1/4" T-Nut

MATERIALS LIST

Part	Quantity	Dimensions
Base	1	12" × 24" – 3/4"
Fence	1	4" × 24" – 3/4"
Clamp block	1	1 3/4" × 3" – 3/4" hardwood
Toggle clamp	1	6 1/2" × 1 3/4" low silhouette
Threaded stud	1	1/4" threads, 1 1/2"-long stud
Washer	1	1/4"
T-nuts	6	1/4"

Install the T-nuts

With the holes drilled for the T-nuts, you can attach them to the base. Insert a T-nut into each counterbore and tap them in place with a hammer as shown in the top photo. In most cases, the face of your hammer will be too big to fit into the counterbore to fully seat the T-nut. To remedy this, use a stove bolt or carriage bolt as a pin punch along with the hammer to drive the prongs of the T-nut fully into the base to lock it in place.

Attach the fence to the base

The base is complete at this point, so go ahead and attach the fence. If you're using MDF (medium-density fiberboard, as shown here), make sure to drill pilot holes in the fence and into the edge of the base to prevent the screws from splitting the MDF as the screws are driven in (see the left middle photo).

Prepare the clamp block

The clamp block needs five holes drilled into it, as illustrated in the drawing below: a single $1/4$"-diameter one centered on the width of the block and about 1" in from the end for the threaded stud to pass through (as shown in the right middle photo), and four mounting holes for the toggle clamp. To locate these, position the toggle clamp on the end of the block and mark through the holes in the base. Then drill pilot holes for the mounting screws.

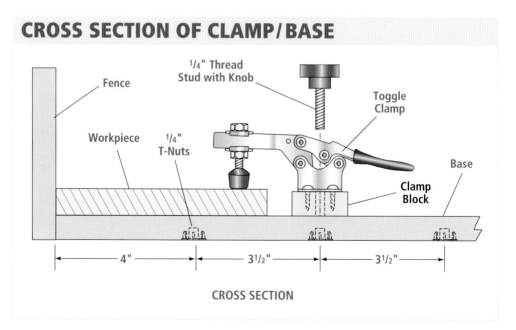

CROSS SECTION OF CLAMP/BASE

Fence

$1/4$" Thread Stud with Knob

Toggle Clamp

Workpiece

$1/4$" T-Nuts

Base

Clamp Block

4"

$3^{1}/_{2}$"

$3^{1}/_{2}$"

CROSS SECTION

Attach the toggle clamp

To complete the clamping block, attach the toggle clamp. Position it on the block and drive in the mounting screws as shown in the top photo.

USING THE MITER SAW TABLE

Before you can use the miter saw table, you'll first need to attach it to your saw and adjust the cutting depth as described below.

Attach the table to your saw. Center the table from side to side on your saw table, and butt the

fence up against the saw's fence. Mark through the holes on the saw's fence on the face of the miter saw table fence. Drill pilot holes and attach the table with #8 × ¾" wood screws.

Clamp the workpiece. Place your workpiece on the saw table and butt it up against the fence. Slide it back and forth until the cut line aligns with the blade. Then choose a T-nut location for the clamping block and secure the

block. Adjust the toggle clamp pad as needed, and toggle the clamp to lock the workpiece in place.

Reset the saw cutting depth. To keep the saw blade from cutting all the way through the base, reset your saw cut depth to cut about ¼" into the base. If your saw doesn't have this feature, you can usually slip a shim between the saw arm and the stop that limits the depth of cut.

Make the cut. All that's left is to make the cut; before you do, double-check to make sure the blade won't hit any T-nut. You'll notice increased precision now that the workpiece can't shift as the blade enters and leaves the workpiece.

Miter Saw Fence

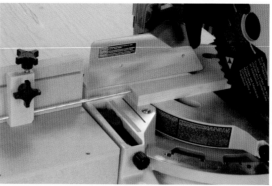

Cutting identical-length parts is a common task for the miter saw. Although you can clamp a scrap to the fence to serve as a stop, you're severely limited in length because of the shortness of the saw table and fence. Some manufacturers try to extend this range with extension wings or tables. Although this does offer better support for the workpiece, it does nothing for the fence. One solution to this problem—especially if you use your saw primarily in the workshop—is to add a miter saw fence to each side of the saw. Yes, you can purchase these—but many offer only an extended fence with no workpiece support. The miter saw fence we designed offers both. What's more, our unique stop block features an extension rod that reaches out over your existing saw table to handle shorter repetitive cuts, as shown in the top photo.

The miter saw fence consists of a front, back, and table, as illustrated in the exploded view on the opposite page. A facing attaches to the back to create a pocket that captures a closet flange bolt used to secure the stop block. An adjustable extension rod passes through the block and is locked in place with a threaded stud.

Cut grooves in the fence
Begin construction by cutting the parts to size per the materials list on the opposite page. Then cut two grooves the length of the back. A shallow groove near the top edge is for the closet flange bolt; the deeper groove accepts the table; see the detail illustration on page 112 for size and locations of these grooves. We cut both grooves on the table saw fitted with a dado blade, as shown in the middle photo. Note: The location of the $3/8$"-deep, $3/4$"-wide groove will depend on the height of your saw's table. Adjust its position accordingly so the table of the miter saw fence will end up flush with the table on your saw.

Glue on the facing
Now you can glue the facing onto the front of the fence. The width/height of this facing will depend on the location of the deeper groove in the fence. Simply measure from the top of the groove to the top of the fence, and cut the facing to match. Apply glue to the fence, taking care to keep it out of the grooves, and clamp the facing in place as shown in the bottom photo.

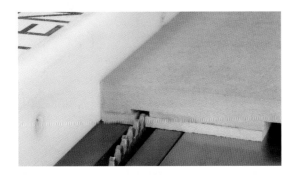

Cut a slot in the facing

To create the pocket for the closet flange bolt that holds the stop block in place, cut a $1/4$"-wide groove in the facing so that it's centered on the width of the groove that the facing covers. You'll want to cut this just slightly wider than $1/4$" so that the closet flange bolt can slide smoothly along the slot. We made the cut on the table saw, as shown in the top photo.

EXPLODED VIEW

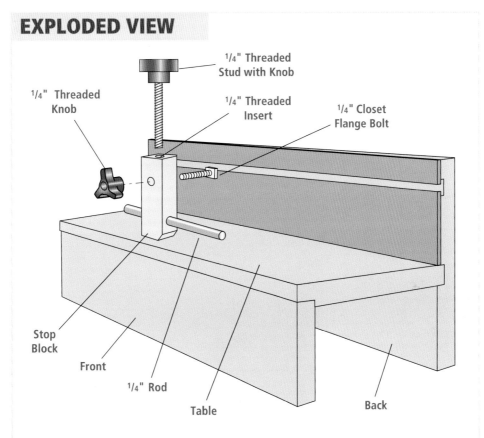

$1/4$" Threaded Stud with Knob

$1/4$" Threaded Knob

$1/4$" Threaded Insert

$1/4$" Closet Flange Bolt

Stop Block

Front

$1/4$" Rod

Table

Back

MATERIALS LIST

Part	Quantity	Dimensions	Part	Quantity	Dimensions
Front	1	$3^{3}/4$" × 24" – $3/4$"	Extension rod	1	$1/4$" diameter, 12" long
Table	1	$6^{3}/4$" × 24" – $3/4$"	Threaded stud	1	$1/4$" threads, 4" long
Back	1	8" × 24" – $3/4$"	Threaded insert	1	$1/4$"
Facing	1	4"* × 24" – $1/4$"	Closet flange bolt	1	$1/4$"
Mounting cleat	1	2" × 20" – $3/4$"	Threaded knob	1	$1/4$" threads
Stop block	1	$1^{3}/4$" × 4" – $3/4$" hardwood	*Width/height of facing will depend on the height of your saw table.		

Rabbet the table

The fence is basically done at this point, so you can turn your attention to the table and front. All that's required here in terms of joinery is a rabbet cut on the bottom front edge of the table to accept the front. We cut the $3/8$"-deep, $3/4$"-wide rabbet on the table saw fitted with a dado blade, as shown in the top left photo.

Assemble the fence

Now you can assemble the fence. Begin by gluing and screwing the table into the groove in the fence. Make sure to drill pilot holes before driving in screws. Then glue and screw the front to the table as shown in the top right photo.

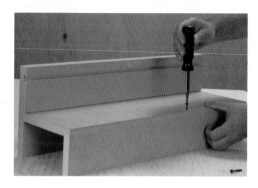

CROSS SECTION OF FENCE AND STOP BLOCK

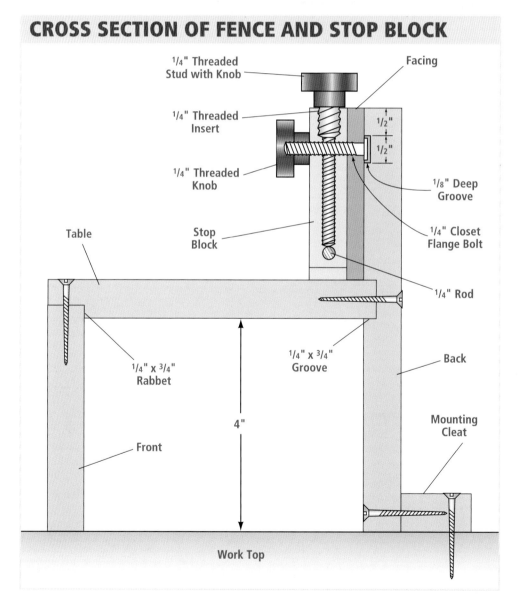

$1/4$" Threaded Stud with Knob

$1/4$" Threaded Insert

$1/4$" Threaded Knob

Facing

$1/2$"

$1/2$"

$1/8$" Deep Groove

$1/4$" Closet Flange Bolt

Table

Stop Block

$1/4$" Rod

$1/4$" x $3/4$" Rabbet

$1/4$" x $3/4$" Groove

Back

Front

4"

Mounting Cleat

Work Top

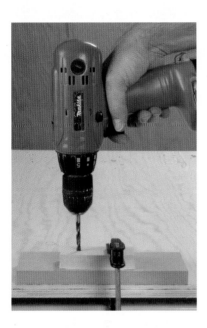

Drill a mounting hole in the stop

With the fence assembled, the next step is to make the stop block. Start by drilling a $1/4$" mounting hole in the stop as shown in the top photo. This hole is centered on the width of the stop and is $3/4$" down from the top edge.

Drill holes for the extension rod

Next, flip the stop over onto its side and locate and drill the hole for the extension rod as shown in the middle photo. This $1/4$" hole is centered on the thickness of the stop and is $1/2$" up from the bottom edge. Then position the stop on its end and drill the long hole needed for the extension lock (see the detail drawing on the opposite page). If your drill bit isn't long enough to drill this in one pass, flip the stop over and drill in through the bottom to connect the holes. The extension lock hole is centered on the thickness of the stop and is $1/2$" in from the side of the stop. Finally, you'll need to enlarge the extension lock hole in the top of the stop for the threaded insert that accepts the lock. The size of this hole will depend on the insert you're using.

Install the threaded insert

Once all the holes are drilled in the stop, you can start adding the hardware. Start by installing the threaded insert in the top of the stop for the extension lock. Although we frequently use the pound-in style of threaded insert, this jig calls for one with exterior threads. If you use a pound-in insert, it will be forced out of the hole when you tighten the extension lock as the threaded stud is tightened against the extension rod.

Attach stop to the fence

Next you can attach the stop to the fence. The hardware for this consists of an ordinary closet flange bolt (sometimes referred to as "Johnny" bolts, as they're used to secure a toilet to its closet flange), a washer, and a threaded knob. Slide the flanged end of the closet bolt into the pocket groove in the fence, slip on the stop and washer, and install the threaded knob as shown in the top photo.

Add the extension rod

The extension rod is just a 12"-length of steel rod with the ends smoothed and chamfered slightly with a file. Slip the rod into the horizontal hole near the bottom of the stop, as shown in the middle photo. If it sticks, either enlarge the hole slightly or apply a bit of paraffin to the rod, or do both.

Install the extension lock

The extension lock is a threaded stud with $1/4$" threads that are 4" long. If you can't find one of these, you can make your own by cutting a $4^{1}/_{2}$" to 5" length of threaded rod and locking it into a $1/4$" threaded knob with a $1/4$" jam nut. Thread the extension lock down into the threaded insert in the top of the stop until it contacts the extension rod, as shown in the bottom photo.

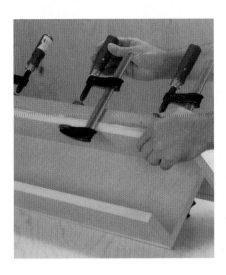

Add a mounting cleat

To keep the miter saw fence from shifting around when it's in place next to your saw, you'll want to add a mounting cleat to the bottom outside edge of the fence back. Drill pilot holes for the mounting screws before you glue and clamp the mounting cleat to the back as shown in the top left photo.

Attach the fence to your work surface

Now you can secure the fence to your work surface. Position the fence so the facing is in line with the fence on your saw and then drive screws through the mounting cleat and into your work surface to lock it in place, as shown in the top right photo.

USING THE STOP BLOCK

The stop block for the miter saw fence can be used in two modes: standard and extended.

Standard mode. In standard mode, the extension rod is not used with the stop block; the stop is simply positioned along the fence and locked in place to define the length of the cut.

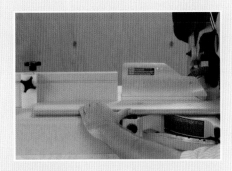

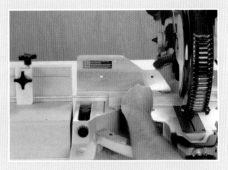

Extension mode. With the extension mode, the stop block is positioned near the saw table and the extension rod is inserted, adjusted over, and locked in place to define the length of the cut.

Wide-Angle Jig

The miter angle on most miter saws is adjustable from 45 degrees left to 45 degrees right—some saws offer a slightly increased range such as 50 degrees to 50 degrees. This is fine for most cuts, but what do you do when you need a workpiece cut to a 60-degree or 75-degree angle? A common unsafe practice is to position the end of the workpiece against the fence and make a cut. A better, safer, more accurate solution is to use a wide-angle jig like the shop-made version shown in the top photo.

This jig is really just a positioning guide for your workpiece. For added safety, we attached a toggle clamp to lock your workpiece in place for the cut. The wide-angle jig consists of a base, a clamping bar, and a guide strip with a toggle clamp, as illustrated in the exploded view on the opposite page.

Attach clamping bar to the base
To make the wide-angle jig, begin by cutting the parts to size per the materials list on the opposite page. Then attach the clamping bar to the front edge of the base with glue and screws as shown in the middle photo.

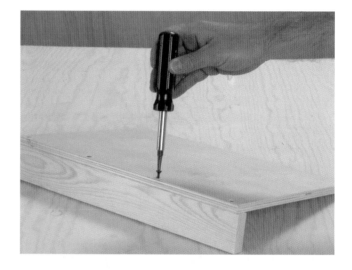

Attach the guide strip
The next step is to attach the guide strip to the base. One end butts up against the fence, and the strip is located about 4" in from the right edge of the base. Attach the guide strip with glue and screws as shown in the bottom photo. Take care to align this so it's absolutely perpendicular to the clamping bar.

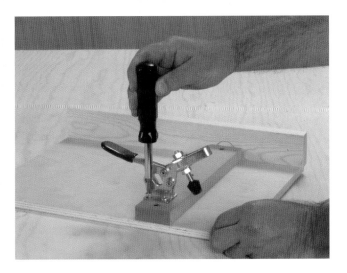

Attach the toggle clamp

To complete the wide-angle jig, attach a toggle clamp to the guide strip as shown in the top photo. Position the outer edge of the base of the clamp about 1" in from the end of the guide strip (see the detail drawing on the bottom of page 118). Locate the mounting holes by positioning the toggle clamp on the end of the guide, and mark through the holes in the base. Then drill pilot holes for the mounting screws and drive in the screws.

EXPLODED VIEW

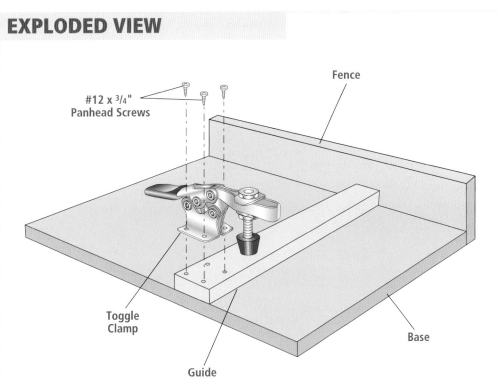

#12 x ³/₄"
Panhead Screws

Fence

Toggle
Clamp

Guide

Base

MATERIALS LIST		
Part	Quantity	Dimensions
Base	1	12" × 16" – ¹/₂" plywood
Fence	1	2" × 16" – ³/₄"
Guide	1	2" × 11¹/₄" – ³/₄"
Toggle clamp	1	6¹/₂" × 1³/₄", low silhouette

USING THE JIG

Using the wide-angle jig is simple; all that you have to keep in mind is that the jig basically rotates your saw's fence 90 degrees. This means you end up with a complementary angle of the setting on your miter saw. So when your saw is set to 10 degrees, the jig provides you with an 80-degree cut; a 15-degree saw setting results in a 75-degree cut.

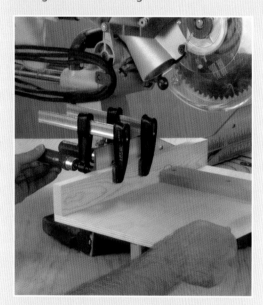

Reset the cutting depth. To prevent your saw blade from cutting all the way through the base of the jig, reset your saw cut depth to cut about ¼" into the base, as shown in the top photo. If your saw doesn't have this feature, you can usually slip a shim between the saw arm and the stop that limits the depth of cut.

Clamp the jig to the saw. To use the wide-angle jig, start by positioning it on your saw. Butt the clamping bar up against your fence and adjust the jig from side to side to position your workpiece for the desired cut. Then clamp the jig to your saw by spanning the clamping bar and saw fence with clamps as shown.

CROSS SECTION OF JIG/CLAMP

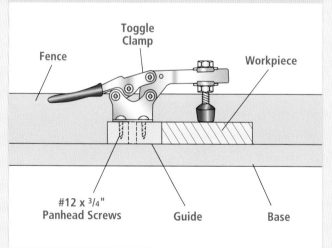

Fence • Toggle Clamp • Workpiece • #12 x ³/₄" Panhead Screws • Guide • Base

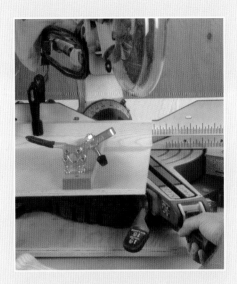

Select the angle. Now you can select the cut angle and adjust your saw accordingly, as shown in the top left photo. Remember, the jig provides a complementary angle. So a 20-degree setting on your saw will result in a 70-degree cut angle.

Clamp the workpiece. With the jig in place and the angle set, you can position and clamp your workpiece to the jig. For the toggle clamp to hold the work securely, you may need to adjust the position and the height of the clamp pad as shown in the top right inset photo. This is easily accomplished by loosening the two nuts on the threaded shaft of the clamp, repositioning the pad, and then retightening the nuts. Then simply toggle the clamp to lock the workpiece in place as shown in the top middle photo.

Make the cut. Finally, lower the blade into the workpiece to make the cut, as shown in the bottom photo. Use a slow feed rate to prevent the blade from digging in and twisting the workpiece as it starts the cut.

6 Miter Saw Repair and Maintenance

Unlike larger power tools (like table saws), where you often need to crawl under a table top or inside a cabinet to maintain or repair the tool, the bulk of the parts and adjustments on a miter saw are readily accessible. Add to this the fact that many of the adjustments and repairs are straightforward—and that most saw makers provide decent instructions in their owner's manual—and you'll find that keeping your miter saw tuned and running in perfect condition is fairly simple.

With this in mind, it might surprise you that this is one of the longest chapters in this book. Why? Much has to do with the variety of miter saws available—we wanted to make sure to cover chop saws, compound miter saws, and sliding compound miter saws, along with the myriad accessories you can add to increase the performance of your saw (like an add-on fence and laser guides). Then we finish the chapter with common problems that you're likely to face, along with their solutions.

It doesn't take a lot of fancy tools and supplies to maintain a miter saw. You'll need your owner's manual, some cleaning supplies and lubricants, and a few common hand tools.

Inspection

One of the best habits you can get into with respect to your miter saw is to inspect before you use it. This not only helps maintain the life of the tool, but it also protects you from working with an unsafe tool. Look for loose screws, misalignment, binding or moving parts, broken parts, or damage to the cord. When you power up the saw, pay particular attention to how it feels and sounds. If you notice any odd vibration or noise, stop at once. Don't use the saw until it has been checked out and repaired. A more thorough inspection, like the one described here, can be made less frequently.

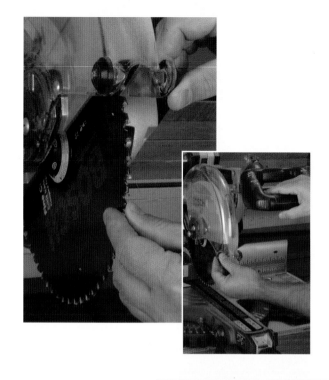

Blade and guard

The first thing to check on a miter saw is the blade and guard. To do this, lower the blade with the power off to see if the guard retracts and returns to its proper position. Then grip the guard and pivot it back and forth to make sure it pivots smoothly (top inset photo). If it binds, check the linkage and lubricate if needed (see page 126). Again, with the power off, lift up the guard and slowly rotate the blade a full 360 degrees as shown in the top photo. Look for cracks in the blade and chipped or missing teeth, and replace the blade if you find either.

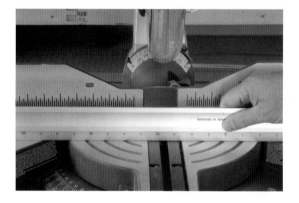

Table

Just like the top of a table saw, the saw table on a miter saw should be inspected routinely to make sure it's flat. The simplest way to do this is to place a known-straight straightedge on its edge on the top and shine a low-angle light behind the straightedge, as shown in the bottom left photo. If you see light, it indicates a low spot in the table. The low spot shown here is common—it's directly under the kerf plate or inserts. This can be remedied by shimming under the plate or inserts with tape or thin washers.

Stops

Once you've checked the table, take a quick look to make sure any built-in stops are working properly. Pivot or rotate the stops as required, and make sure that they lock positively in place, as shown in the bottom right photo.

Table and bevel pivots

Next, rotate the table to various angles to make sure the detents lock in positively and that the table pivots smoothly, as shown in the top photo. See pages 127–130 for more on checking and adjusting stops, and pages 140–141 for information on maintaining the pivot mechanism. Then loosen the bevel lock and tilt the blade through its full range of motion to be sure it tilts smoothly and the stops are accurate.

Hold-downs

It's also a good idea to check any hold-downs to make sure they will lock a workpiece in place. The simplest way to do this is to position a long workpiece against the fence and lock it in place with a hold-down. Then just tug on the end of the workpiece as shown in the middle photo. If the hold-down is doing its job, the workpiece won't budge.

Fence

Finally, check the saw fence. Butt a small engineer's square or the head of a combination square up against the fence as shown in the bottom photo. There should be no gaps between the blade and the fence. If there are, take your saw to a local machine shop to have the fence reground. Alternatively, you can purchase a replacement fence from the manufacturer. (For more on adjusting a saw fence, see page 131.)

Cleaning

To keep a miter saw running in peak condition, it's important to routinely clean the saw. How often you clean your miter saw will depend on how frequently you use it. In some shops, a saw may need daily cleaning; in others, once a week or once a month is plenty.

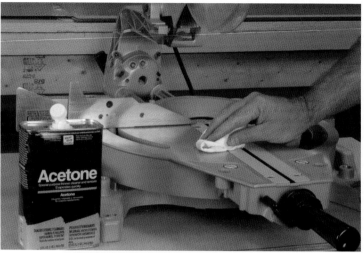

Table

If you've applied a sealer to the table to prevent rust and to help workpieces glide smoothly over the surface, you should start by cleaning the table with a clean cloth dipped in solvent, such as the acetone shown in the top photo. This will remove any old sealant or other impurities on the saw top. Always check your solvent in an inconspicuous place to make sure it won't damage the top—and stay clear of any plastic, which is notorious for clouding when it comes in contact with most solvents.

If there is pitch and resin (or other goo) buildups on your saw table, the acetone may not take these off. If you run into stubborn areas like this, try scrubbing them off with a non-abrasive pad or a piece of fine silicon-carbide sandpaper dipped in the solvent, as shown in the middle photo. If this doesn't remove it, see page 136 for more-aggressive measures.

Detents

The detents of your saw table will benefit from a routine cleaning. How you clean them will depend on what style they are. The most common style has notches below the table. Sawdust and chips can build up in these, resulting in inaccurate angles. A brass-bristle brush will quickly remove any buildup with a quick scrubbing, as shown in the bottom photo.

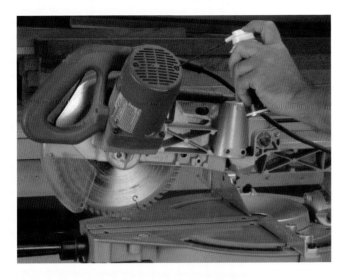

Motor

The motors on all miter saws have vents in their sides to promote air circulation to keep the motor cool. Unfortunately, along with the air that gets circulated comes dust. When dust builds up inside the motor housing—particularly when it attaches itself to the motor windings—it acts as an insulator to keep heat in— just the opposite of what you want. That's why it's important to routinely blow out your motor housing with a blast of compressed or canned air, as shown in the top photo.

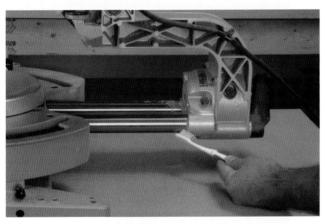

Slides (if applicable)

If your miter saw is the sliding compound variety, you'll want to keep the slides free from dust and chip buildup. Since these slides are typically lubricated, the mixture of dust and the lubricant can often result in a thick goo, which can foul the slides. This is easily removed with an old toothbrush, as shown in the middle photo. Accumulations like this typically build up at the limits of the slides (for more on maintaining slides, see page 139).

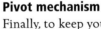

Pivot mechanism

Finally, to keep your pivot mechanism pivoting smoothly, you should routinely give it a blast of compressed or canned air as shown in the bottom photo. Access may be limited, depending on your saw, but it's usually possible to get in close enough to blow out most debris (for more on maintaining the pivot mechanism, see pages 140–141).

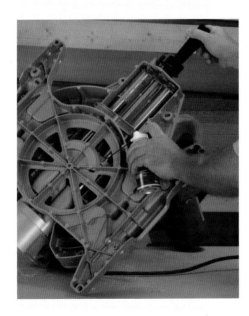

Lubrication

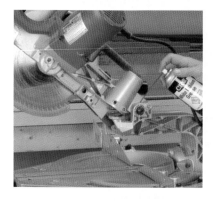

One of the best ways to keep your miter saw running in tip-top shape is to lubricate key moving parts periodically. There's definitely a Catch-22 with lubrication, however: You need to keep parts lubricated—but oil and grease attract dust. When you combine sawdust with oil or grease, you soon end up with a thick goo that can slow down parts and interfere with stops. That's why it's so important to keep your saw clean inside and out. Before you lubricate a single part, take the time to clean it first; see pages 124–125. If you don't first remove the existing goo, your lubricant will be ineffective. Parts on the saw that need periodic lubrication include the blade guard linkages, saw table and sliding fence, carriage pivot, tilt mechanism, table pivot and lock, and slides (if applicable), as illustrated in the drawing at right.

Carriage pivot

The carriage pivot—the main pivot that allows the saw to pivot up and down—requires the most frequent lubrication. After you've cleaned the pivot thoroughly, apply some white lithium grease sparingly. We prefer the spray-on type with a long applicator tube, as shown in the top left photo, so we can get the lubricant exactly where we need it without worry of overspray. Make sure to wipe off any excess to prevent the sawdust from attaching itself to the lubricant.

Table pivot

The table pivot is the next part that will require frequent lubrication, as it's constantly being pivoted to various angles. Here again, we use spray-on white lithium grease for this, as it's the easiest to apply in close quarters (top right photo). For more on maintaining the pivot mechanism, see pages 140–141.

LUBRICATION POINTS

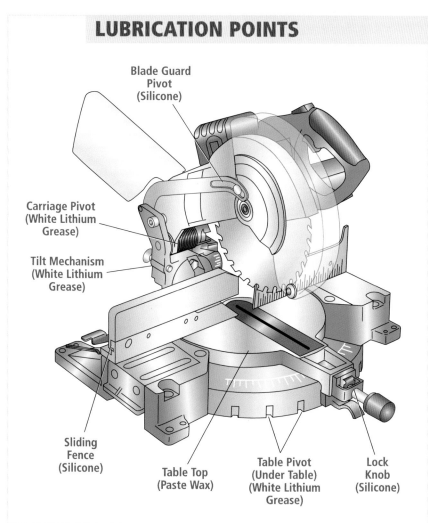

Blade Guard Pivot (Silicone)

Carriage Pivot (White Lithium Grease)

Tilt Mechanism (White Lithium Grease)

Sliding Fence (Silicone)

Table Top (Paste Wax)

Table Pivot (Under Table) (White Lithium Grease)

Lock Knob (Silicone)

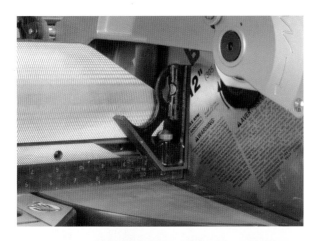

Adjusting the Blade Square to the Table

For the bulk of your crosscuts, you'll want the saw blade to be square to the table. On virtually every miter saw we've come across, the 90-degree stop is adjustable—and it's a fairly straightforward adjustment, as described below. Check your owner's manual for the specific alignment procedure for your saw.

Check the alignment
To adjust the saw blade so it's square to the table, start by checking its alignment. Butt the head of a combination square (or small engineer's square) up against the blade as shown in the top photo. If there are any gaps between the square head, the blade of the square, and the table, the 90-degree stop needs aligning; see below.

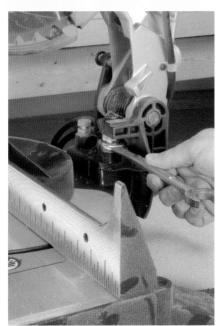

Adjust the stop
Most 90-degree stops are located on one or both sides of the carriage pivot. The stop itself is usually the head of a large bolt that's locked in place with a jam nut. To adjust the stop, first loosen the jam nut as shown in the middle photo. Then adjust the stop bolt until there are no gaps between the square head, the blade, and the table. Tighten the jam nut and recheck the alignment. Readjust as needed to eliminate any gaps.

Align the indicator
Once the 90-degree stop is adjusted, you'll likely need to realign the miter-bevel angle indicator. This is typically held in place with a screw. Loosen the screw to friction-tight and then adjust the position of the indicator so it points exactly to zero, as shown in the bottom photo. Tighten the screw and make sure the indicator doesn't shift as the screw is tightened. Perform the quick accuracy test described on page 45 to verify that the blade is square to the table.

Adjusting Miter Stops

The miter stops or miter detent locations are typically milled into the frame of the table base and are set at the factory. This means that on most saws they are not adjustable. What is adjustable, however, is the miter angle indicator; see below. Check your owner's manual for the specific adjustment procedure (if any) for your saw.

Check the alignment

The first thing to do is check your miter alignment. Start by pivoting your saw to one of the 45-degree stops and lock it in place. Then use an accurate reference tool to test the alignment. Although you can use the angled head of a combination square for this, we prefer the wider reference surfaces that a speed square offers. Just butt the square between the blade and the fence as shown in the top photo. There should be no gaps between the edges of the square and the blade and fence. If there are, the detent is off and you'll need to either return the saw to an authorized factory service center for repair or else override the detent and not use it anymore. If this is possible on your saw, override the detent and adjust the pivot angle until the gaps are eliminated and lock the table in place with the miter-lock handle.

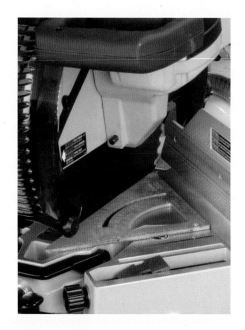

Adjust the indicator

With the blade at exactly 45 degrees, loosen the miter indicator screw to friction-tight and adjust the position of the indicator until its hairline is exactly over the 45-degree mark, as shown in the middle photo. Retighten the screw and double-check the alignment.

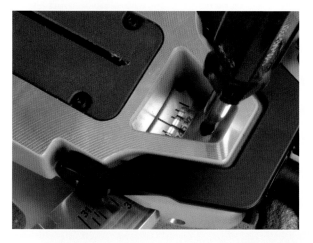

Verify the alignment

Once you've aligned the indicator, pivot the saw over to the other 45-degree stop and check the alignment on that side with a speed square or the head of a combination square. Here again, there should be no gaps and the indicator hairline should read exactly 45 degrees. If there are gaps and/or the indicator reads an angle other than 45 degrees, return the saw to the manufacturer for repair.

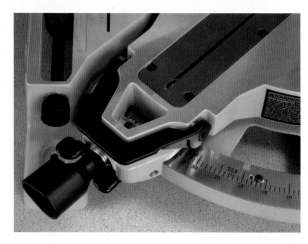

Adjusting Bevel Stops

Once you've checked and aligned the 90-degree stop (as described on page 127), it's a good idea to check the 45-degree bevel stop (or stops) as well. A 45-degree stop is similar to a 90-degree stop in terms of location and adjustment—except it'll be on the other side of the carriage pivot.

Check the alignment

To adjust the 45-degree bevel stop (or stops), start by checking its alignment. The head of a combination square works well for this. Loosen the bevel lock and tilt the blade until it hits the 45-degree stop and tighten the bevel lock. Then butt the angled head of the combination square up against the blade as shown in the top photo. There should be no gap between the head of the square and the blade. If there is, you'll need to adjust the stop.

Adjust the stop

Like the 90-degree stop, the 45-degree stop is typically the head of a large bolt that's locked in place with a jam nut. To adjust the stop, start by loosening the jam nut to friction-tight, as shown in the middle photo. Then use a wrench to adjust the stop itself to eliminate the gap between the head of the square and the blade. Tighten the jam nut and recheck the alignment, readjusting it as needed. Repeat for the opposite stop if your saw tilts in both directions.

Check the indicator

Once you've adjusted the stop, it's a good idea to check the bevel indicator to make sure it points to 45 degrees. If it doesn't—and you previously aligned it to read 0 degrees—the scale itself is likely off and you'll need to return the saw to the manufacturer for repair. Do not adjust the indicator, as then it won't read correctly at 0 degrees—or at any other angle, for that matter.

Adjusting the Fit between the Table and Base

Since the tables on most miter saws are constantly being pivoted to the left and right to make various angled cuts, it's important that the fit between the table and the base create a pivoting action that is smooth, yet accurate. This means there can't be any play or slop in the mechanism. On some saws, this action can be adjusted by the owner. On others, you'll need to take the saw into a factory-authorized service center for this adjustment. Check your owner's manual to see if there's an adjustment procedure for this.

Pivot mechanisms 101

Before you adjust a pivot mechanism, it's important to understand how the basic system works. On most saws, there is a central pivot shaft that connects the table to the base (the dark shaft protruding from the underside of the table in the top photo). This shaft passes through a hole in the base and is held in place by a lock nut that may or may not be accessible. A set of columns on the underside of the table terminate in pads (note the four columns in the top photo with the dark circular pads) that mate with a smooth arced surface milled into the top of the base. The fit between these pads and the milled surface will determine how smoothly the pivot mechanism operates.

Check the action

The pivot mechanism on your saw should pivot smoothly from side to side, as long as the pivot or miter lock is disengaged. Test the action to verify that it's smooth, as shown in the bottom left photo. If it feels too tight or too loose, check your owner's manual for an adjustment procedure.

Adjust the fit

In most cases, the fit between the table and the base is adjusted by varying how firmly the lock nut pulls the table-mounted shaft into the base. Frequently all that's required to adjust the fit is to flip the saw over (with the power disconnected) and rotate the lock nut, as shown in the bottom right photo. Adjust the nut, check the action, and repeat until you have a smooth pivot with no play. If you find that the action "catches" or is rough, the mechanism may need more work; see pages 140–141.

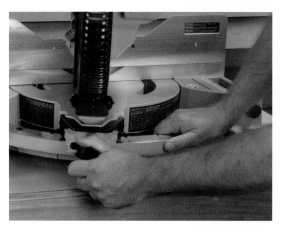

Adjusting the Fences

An improperly aligned fence can lead to inaccurate cuts. Fortunately, it's easy to both check and align most miter saw fences.

Check the alignment

When a fence is properly aligned, it is perfectly perpendicular to the blade. Although you may not notice a misaligned fence when cutting narrow stock, it'll be more obvious with wider stock. To check alignment, just butt the head of a combination square (or a try square) up against the fence and blade as shown in the top photo. There should be no gap between the square and the fence or the blade. If there is, you'll need to correct this. Check your owner's manual for the adjustment procedure. In most cases it'll be similar to that described below.

Loosen the fence bolts to friction-tight

If your fence is out of alignment, start by loosening the fence-mounting bolts to friction-tight, as shown in the middle photo. There are typically two or four of these, and they may be bolts or machine screws with hex heads, slotted heads, or heads that accept an Allen wrench. Take care here to loosen them only enough to adjust the fence.

Adjust the fence

With the fence bolts loosened to friction-tight, pivot the fence as needed to eliminate any gaps between the square, fence, and blade, as shown in the bottom photo. Recheck the alignment and if it's good, tighten the bolts and check one more time; tightening the bolts can often rack the fence out of alignment. If it's not aligned, repeat this procedure as necessary until it comes into alignment. Then re-tighten the bolts to lock the newly aligned fence in place.

Changing Blades

Although you might think changing a blade on a miter saw is intuitive, it's not. That's because the blade guard, along with its linkage, gets in the way of the arbor shaft nut that locks the blade in place. The location and type of the guard bracket hardware vary from saw to saw. Check your owner's manual for blade-changing instructions. Make sure to unplug your saw whenever you change a blade.

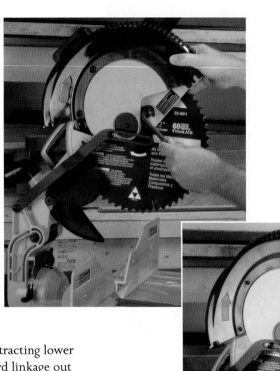

Loosen the guard bracket hardware

On virtually any miter saw that has a retracting lower guard, you'll first need to pivot the guard linkage out of the way to expose the arbor nut. There's either a screw or bolt that holds this in place, and what you want to do is loosen it only enough to lift the guard linkage out of the way, as shown in the top photo. Do not remove this screw or nut, as it can be a hassle to get back in place.

Expose the arbor nut

Once you've loosened the screw or bolt sufficiently, lift the lower guard all the way up as shown in the middle photo. This will expose the arbor nut so that you can loosen it in the next step.

Loosen the nut and remove the blade

Almost all miter saws now have a shaft lock button that you depress to keep the arbor shaft from rotating as you loosen the arbor nut. Locate and depress this and use the manufacturer-supplied wrench to loosen the arbor nut or bolt, as shown in the bottom photo (since this is a reverse-thread screw, you'll want to turn the nut or bolt in a clockwise direction to loosen it). Remove the nut or bolt and the outer flange. Then lift off the blade. Reverse this procedure to install a blade—just make sure the teeth on the new blade point back toward the fence at the bottom of the blade.

Cleaning Blades

Miter saw blades require regular maintenance. Although carbide-tipped blades need much less frequent sharpening than high-speed steel (HSS) blades, both types will cut truer and last longer if kept clean.

A blade-cleaning kit

Over time, saw blades will pick up pitch and gum from the woods you cut. If you cut a lot of softwoods, the blades can pick up a lot of resin as well. Any of these buildups on your saw blades will decrease the cutting efficiency of the blades and also tend to cause burning and ragged cuts. To promote blade cleaning, consider making a blade-cleaning kit consisting of an old or disposable pizza pan, an old toothbrush, rubber gloves, and a can of pitch and gum remover, as shown in the top photo. Keep a couple of old newspapers on hand as well to protect surrounding work surfaces.

Spray on the cleaner

To clean a blade, put on a pair of rubber gloves and place the blade in the pizza pan. Carefully spray on a coat of pitch and gum remover, as shown in the photo second from top. Make sure to wear eye protection here, as this stuff is pretty toxic.

Brush the teeth

After the pitch and gum remover has sat for the recommended time, scrub the teeth with an old toothbrush, as shown in the photo at left, to remove stubborn deposits.

Wipe the blade clean

Wipe off any chemical residue with a clean cloth, flip the blade, and clean the other side, as shown in the bottom photo. When done, wipe both sides and clean one more time. If rust is a problem in your shop, consider spraying on a sealer such as DriCote to keep out moisture.

Sharpening Blades

With use, miter saw blades will dull and need sharpening. Although we generally recommend that you have this done professionally, there are a few instances where sharpening a blade yourself can save you time and money. In particular, in case you accidentally hit something (a really tough knot or a piece of hardware), it pays to know how to touch up a dull tooth or two. If all the teeth are dull, drop the blade off at a sharpening service and have it sharpened by a pro.

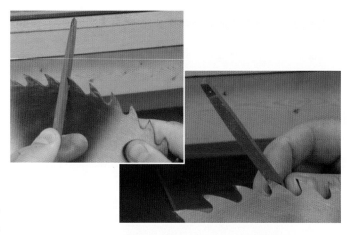

High-speed steel blades

Just like any other high-speed steel blade in your workshop (like a handsaw), a HSS saw blade can be sharpened with a slim taper file, like the one shown in the top photos. Here again, we advise you to have this done professionally because if you don't sharpen every tooth identically and set each alternate tooth perfectly, the blade will not run true. Touch-up sharpening can be done by pressing a file against the tooth so it aligns with the bevel, as shown in the top left photo. Then take one or two passes with the file to create a fresh edge as shown in the top right photo. Since round saw blades are hard to hold for sharpening without damaging the teeth, consider making a blade clamp as illustrated in the drawing.

Carbide-tipped blades

Carbide-tipped blades are best sharpened by a professional with experience working with carbide. If you don't know of a local sharpener, consult a local woodworking club. Don't use a sharpening service that has not been recommended by a woodworker. If the shop doesn't have the specialized equipment needed to hone a carbide-tipped blade, they can ruin it. And with many blades running easily over $100, you would not be happy. Alternatively, some saw blade makers and mail-order woodworking suppliers offer sharpening service. If you notice a chip or a slightly dull tooth, you can freshen the edge by filing the flats with a diamond hone, as shown in the middle photo.

HOLDER FOR SHARPENING BLADES

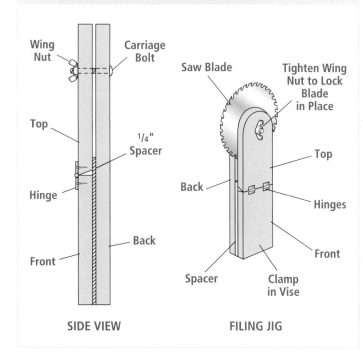

Wing Nut · Carriage Bolt · Top · 1/4" Spacer · Hinge · Back · Front

SIDE VIEW

Saw Blade · Tighten Wing Nut to Lock Blade in Place · Top · Back · Hinges · Front · Spacer · Clamp in Vise

FILING JIG

Storing Blades

Quality miter saw blades—especially carbide-tipped blades with high teeth counts—are expensive. One way to increase the life of your saw blades and protect your investment is to store them properly when they're not being used.

All the methods described below keep the teeth of one saw blade from coming in contact with another. The worst thing you can do is allow blades to lie on top of one another or hang them on a wall. When high-speed steel teeth touch, they dull, and the teeth of carbide-tipped blades can fracture or chip.

Store them in their original jackets

The simplest way to store miter saw blades when not in use is to return them to their original jackets or packaging. Quality blades (like the Bosch blades shown in the top photo) come with sturdy, reusable packaging, as the blade manufacturer is well aware of your investment and wants to help you keep your blades in tip-top condition.

Make a stackable holder

If you no longer have your original blade packaging, or the packaging wasn't reusable or sturdy, you can make a stackable holder like the one shown in the middle photo. This holder is just a scrap of plywood with a $5/8$" dowel set into its center. To keep the blades separated—and the teeth from touching— small wood "donuts" are slipped in between blades. These are easy to make from $1/4$" scrap plywood and a hole saw.

Build a blade case

The next step up in blade storage is to build a case from scrapwood, like the one illustrated in the bottom drawing. The carcase of the case is cut from $3/4$" plywood or MDF, and $1/4$" plywood is used for the dividers. This simple case guarantees that your blades will not come in contact with each other and that the saw teeth will be protected.

SIMPLE BLADE STORAGE

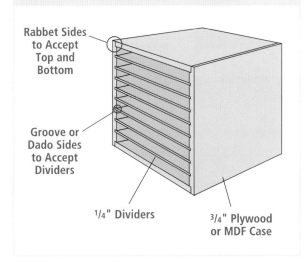

Rabbet Sides to Accept Top and Bottom

Groove or Dado Sides to Accept Dividers

$1/4$" Dividers

$3/4$" Plywood or MDF Case

Maintaining the Saw Table

Since every cut you make on a miter saw involves sliding a workpiece across the table to position it for a cut, it's important to keep the saw table maintained. In addition to helping workpieces slide smoothly, a properly maintained table will help ensure accurate cuts. Additionally, by sealing the table, you'll keep it rust-free.

Checking for flatness

To maintain your saw table, start by making sure that it's flat. Place a level or straightedge across the table and shine a low-angle light behind it as shown in the middle photo. If you see light, it indicates a low spot in the table. You'll often find a low spot directly under the kerf plate or inserts. This can be remedied by shimming under the plate or inserts with tape or thin washers. If there are low spots on the table, you'll need to take it to a local machine shop and have it reground flat.

Smoothing the table

If you've ever applied a sealer to the table to prevent rust and to help workpieces glide smoothly over the surface, you should start by cleaning the table with a clean cloth dipped in solvent, such as acetone. This will remove any old sealant or other impurities on the saw top. Always check your solvent in an inconspicuous place to make sure it won't damage the top—and stay clear of any plastic, which is notorious for clouding when it comes in contact with most solvents. Once the top has been cleaned, it's good

practice to follow this with an abrasive pad. Rub a pad across the entire surface of the saw table (as shown in the bottom left photo) to abrade away any rust or other minor surface imperfections.

Flattening a table

Occasionally, you'll come across heavy rust spots or other buildups that won't come off with the abrasive pad. In cases like this, you'll need to step up to a more aggressive abrasive. Emery cloth or silicon-carbide sandpaper wrapped around a scrap block or sanding block will do a good job of leveling most buildups and removing heavy rust, as shown in the bottom right photo. Start with a coarse grit (such as 100) and work up to around 320-grit to remove the scratches on the table left by the prior grit. Another product that's useful here is rubber-bonded abrasive blocks sold under the Sandflex brand name (available at www.woodcraft.com). They come in fine, medium, and coarse grits and do a great job of removing rust from saw tables.

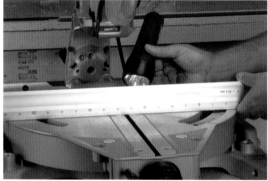

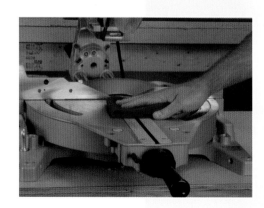

Paste wax

It's an old standard and it still works well—paste wax for a table top. Although there are newer spray-on lubricants and sealers (see below), paste wax does a good job of sealing your table and helping wood slide over it smoothly. Wipe on a generous coat with a clean cloth, as shown in the top photo, and then buff it to a dull sheen.

Spray-on sealers

There are a number of excellent saw table sealers available that will seal your freshly cleaned and de-rusted table. Most of these also leave a dry lubricant on the surface that promotes smooth cuts by helping workpieces glide effortlessly on the saw table. The two that we've had the most luck with are TopCote and Boeshield T-9. Both are simply sprayed on the table as shown in the middle photo. Note: Before you spray, it's a good idea to thoroughly vacuum your saw table to remove any dirt, dust, or leftover sanding grit—you don't want to seal this into the table.

After you've sprayed on the sealant, allow it to completely dry and then buff the saw table with a clean, dry cloth as shown in the bottom photo. You should see a noticeably higher sheen, and your workpieces will now glide smoothly on the saw table.

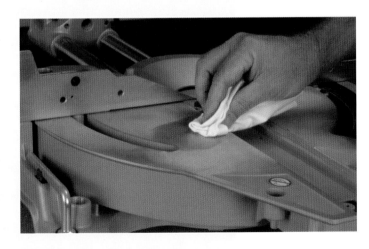

Maintaining Kerf Plates and Inserts

To prevent your workpiece from splintering as the blade passes through a workpiece, saw manufacturers set kerf plates or kerf inserts into the table top. When adjusted and maintained properly, these inserts back up the wood fibers on the underside of the workpiece to prevent chip-out and splintering. Kerf plates are typically a single piece of molded plastic and are not adjustable; separate kerf inserts can be adjusted individually to handle a variety of cuts.

Adjusting kerf inserts

For all cuts where the blade is 90 degress to the table, kerf inserts should be adjusted as close to the blade as possible to provide maximum support to the workpiece, to help prevent splintering. Since most blades are $1/8$" thick, you can use a piece of $1/8$" hardboard as a handy spacer to adjust the gap between the inserts, as shown in the far right photo—just make sure that the hardboard is centered directly below the blade when you adjust the inserts. For bevel cuts, where the blade is titled, you'll need to widen the gap to prevent the blade from chewing up the inserts—something that cannot be avoided with a kerf plate.

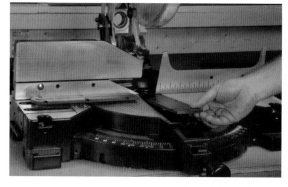

Replacing kerf plates

Over time both kerf inserts and kerf plates can get chewed up and need replacing. This is much more common with kerf plates, as you'll inevitably widen the kerf with bevel cuts and the plate won't be able to support the bottom of the workpiece as well, and splintering will result. With this in mind, it's a good idea to have a spare kerf plate or two (top photo) on hand.

Shop-made kerf plates

Depending on the type and size of your kerf plate, you may be able to make your own for pennies. If your plate is $1/4$" thick (like the one shown in the bottom photo), you can make your own out of $1/4$" hardboard. Use your existing kerf plate as a template to make a replacement plate. To do this, place your kerf plate on a $1/4$"-thick piece of hardboard and trace around it. Then cut it to rough shape to within $1/8$" of the outline. Next, temporarily attach the kerf plate to the hardboard with double-sided tape. Now you can trim it to exact size with a router fitted with a flush-trim bit.

Maintaining the Slides

If your saw is of the compound sliding variety, the slides will require frequent attention to keep them operating smoothly; see below.

Clean the slides

On sliding compound miter saws, you'll want to keep the slides free from dust and chip buildup so the carriage operates smoothly. Start by brushing or vacuuming the slides to remove any loose debris, as shown in the top photo. Since slides are usually lubricated, the mixture of dust and lubricant will often result in a thick goo, which can foul the slides. This can be removed with an old toothbrush. Accumulations like this typically build up at the limits of the slides.

Smooth if necessary

If you notice a catch or rough spot as you slide the carriage assembly back and forth, carefully inspect the slides for dents, dings, or scratches. Any of these can interfere with the sliding action and can be removed by scrubbing the affected area with a fine-grit silicon-carbide sandpaper, as shown in the middle photo. Larger imperfections may need the more aggressive action of emery cloth. If you use either of these, make sure to thoroughly vacuum the slides to prevent sanding grit from fouling the slide.

Lubricate the slides

Once the slides are clean and smooth, you can lubricate them. We use silicone, graphite, or one of the many "dry" lubricants as shown in the bottom photo. These will not attract sawdust like standard lubricants and are safe to use on the slides without having to worry about goo buildup.

Maintaining the Pivot Mechanism

The pivot mechanism on a saw is used every time you angle the blade—you want it to pivot smoothly with no play. On most saws, there is a central pivot shaft that connects the table to the base. This shaft passes through a hole in the base and is held in place by a lock nut that may or may not be accessible. A set of columns on the underside of the table terminate in pads that mate with a smooth arced surface milled into the top of the base. The fit between these pads and the milled surface will deter-mine how smoothly the pivot mechanism operates. If you find

that your pivot is not smooth, and you're mechani-cally inclined, you can take it apart and inspect the mating surfaces. Alternatively, you can take your saw to an authorized factory service center for repair.

Remove the pivot nut and table bolts
To access the mating surfaces of the pivot mecha-nism, start by unplugging your saw and flipping it upside down on a work surface. Then locate the lock nut that threads onto the pivot shaft and remove it, as shown in the far left photo above. Then locate and remove any additional nuts that secure the base to the table, as shown in the top inset photo. Note that on many saws you'll also have to remove the saw fence from the table of the saw before you can separate the table from the base.

Separate the table from the base
Once all the hardware has been removed, flip the saw right side up and lift the table off of the base, as shown in the middle right photo, and set the table aside upside down.

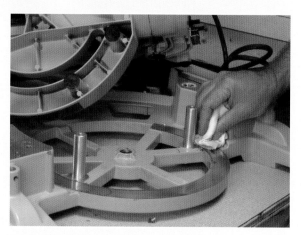

Clean the mating surfaces
Once the mating surfaces of the pivot mechanism are exposed, use a clean soft cloth to clean the pads on the columns on the underside of the table and the arc milled into the base, as shown in the bottom photo.

Inspect the mating surfaces

With the mating surfaces clean, the next step is to inspect them. Although a visual inspection may turn up rough areas, your best bet is to lightly slide your finger slowly along the surface as shown in the top photo. If you find any rough spots or imperfections, mark them with a pencil.

Smooth the surfaces (if necessary)

Small imperfections and scratches that you find on the milled arc's surface can be removed with a silicon-carbide paper wrapped around a small block of wood, as shown in the middle photo. Make sure to use the block to keep the sandpaper from gouging the surface. Large imperfections and deep scratches are best removed by a local machine shop. You'll also want to check the pads on the bottom of the columns. These are often plastic and can also be smoothed with sandpaper wrapped around a scrap block. If you do sand these, take care to keep the block level when sanding, to keep from creating an angled pad.

Lubricate as needed

Once you've smoothed the mating surfaces (if necessary), go back and apply a light coat of lubricant to the arc milled into the table. We like to use white lithium grease in the stick form, as shown in the bottom photo. Wipe off any excess, and reverse the disassembly steps to reassemble the saw. Adjust the lock nut on the pivot shaft to create a smooth pivot with no play.

Installing an Add-On Fence

The fences on miter saws are short, and most are not set up to offer any kind of stop for making repetitive cuts. Fortunately, there are a number of saw makers and accessory manufacturers that offer add-on fences to fit most saws. The add-on fence we're installing here is manufactured by Woodhaven (www.woodhaven.com). The contractor's kit shown here includes two 24" machined fences that mount to the front of your miter saw fence, but are easily removed for transport. Also included are a curved stop, a straight stop, and a track/table extension that provides support for long boards and increases the working length of the fence (you supply the $3/4$"-thick stock for the extension length you want). This kit requires drilling mounting holes in your miter saw fence (but they also offer a no-drill option).

There are also myriad accessories for this fence, including an angle head that mounts to the track that lets you cut 45-degree angles with the saw set at 90 degrees, or cut tapers by angling the saw slightly. You can purchase a crown jig that attaches to the track and holds moldings at the correct angles so all you have to do is make a miter cut. No need to fuss with bevel angles, and it works on either side of the blade. Finally, there's a micro-adjuster that can attach to either stop that allows for precision adjustments.

Check for interference
Place the two tracks on your saw with the pointed ends toward the saw blade, and temporarily clamp them in place. Now adjust your saw to various bevels and angles and check to make sure the tracks do not interfere with the blade or blade guard, as shown in the top photo. Readjust their position as needed until there is no interference.

Install the track-mounting hardware
The two tracks are attached to your saw fence with the mounting hardware provided. There are two mounting options: screw mounting and T-slot mounting. If the holes in your fence are $3/4$", $1^1/2$", or $2^1/4$" up from the table, you can use these for T-slot mounting. If not, you'll need to drill two $9/32$" holes in each fence at one of these heights. Insert the mounting hardware as described in the installation instructions, as shown in the bottom photo. For fences lower than 1" high, you'll need to drill holes in the fence for self-tapping screws (see the installation instructions for more on this).

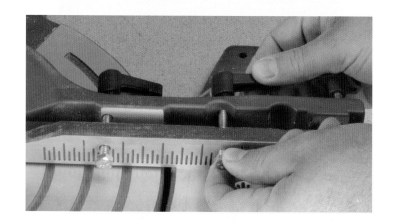

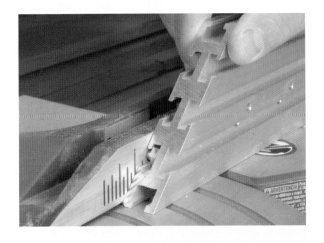

Position the track

Now you can attach the track in front of the existing fence as shown in the top photo. If you're using the T-slot mounting method (as shown here), align the bolt heads with the T-slots in the track and slide them in place.

Adjust the track position and lock in place

When the track is in its final position, secure it to your fences by tightening the spring-loaded knobs as shown in the middle photo. Alternatively, attach the track to your fences with the self-tapping screws provided, driving them through the holes that you drilled previously in your existing fences.

Add the stop and extension (if desired)

With the tracks attached, double-check one more time there they don't interfere with the blade or guard. Now you can add the stop. Some assembly is typically required for these, but they go together in minutes. Slide the head of the mounting bolt into the top slot in the track, and then rotate the knob on top to lock the stop in place as shown in the bottom photo. If you're cutting wide stock or stock that's been cut at an angle on the end, you may want to add an extension to the stop as shown in the bottom inset photo.

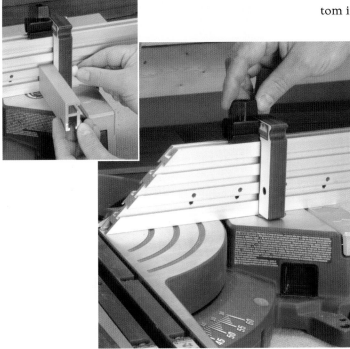

Electrical Repairs

The electrical system of a miter saw is simple and straightforward. Current enters through the plug and continues up the electrical cord. On its way to the motor it passes through the on/off switch. Any of these components can be replaced fairly easily using the manufacturer's replacement part.

Replacing a cord

How readily you can replace an electrical cord depends mostly on the manufacturer. Most manufacturers offer detachable housings that provide relatively easy access. In any case, once the ends of the cord are in sight, make a note of wire colors, locations, and routing. Replace the cord by removing one wire at a time and installing the matching wire of the new cord as shown in the top left photo. This way there won't be any wiring mistakes.

Replacing a power switch

The complexity of replacing a power switch on a miter saw will again depend on the manufacturer and the type of switch you're replacing. Switches vary from toggle switches to micro-switches activated by a plunger. To replace a switch, remove the cover plate and gently pull out the switch. Then note the wire colors and locations before removing the old switch. The most reliable way to replace any power switch is to disconnect one wire at a time and connect it to the corresponding terminal on the replacement switch; see the top right photo.

Accessing the brushes

The brushes in a miter saw provide the means to transfer electrical current to a rotating object (in this case, the armature). Brushes are made up of highly conductive carbon particles pressed together in a small rectangular bar. One end of the brush is curved to match the diameter of the armature. A

spring inserted between an end cap/wire assembly and brush pushes the brush against the armature. By the very nature of this pressing and rubbing action, the brushes will wear down over time. Saw manufacturers provide brush caps on the sides of the motor to access the brushes. Most of these have a slot in the center that accepts a flat-blade screwdriver. With the saw unplugged, insert the screwdriver tip in the slot and rotate the cap until it is loose, as shown in the bottom photo.

Removing the brushes

With the caps removed you can reach in and grab the end cap/spring assembly and pull the brush carefully out as shown in the top photo. As brushes wear and approach the end of their life, you may notice a decrease in power and an accompanying shower of sparks. And if just one brush goes completely bad, the motor will stop. In both situations, the brushes will need replacing; keep in mind that you should always replace brushes in pairs.

Checking the brushes

A healthy brush has a nice even gloss on the end of the brush. If it's scarred, it needs to be replaced. If it's wearing

unevenly, like the brush shown in the middle photo, but no sparks are present, the brush simply may be in its break-in period. Reinstall the brushes and check again after a couple more hours of use. If it's still wearing unevenly, replace the brush, as this means it's not transferring power as efficiently as it should and saw performance will suffer.

Replacing the brushes

As to the length, it's difficult to know when to change brushes unless you know how long they were to start with. As a general rule of thumb, if you've got less than 1/4" left in length (like the left brush in the bottom photo), replace them. Another thing to check brushes for is spring tension. If there isn't enough pressure, the brushes will make intermittent contact and your saw will operate sluggishly. If in doubt, replace them.

Installing Add-On Laser Guides

If your saw doesn't have a laser guide, consider installing an add-on guide. Once you've worked with a miter saw with a laser guide, you won't want to go back to one without a guide. Add-on laser guides are available from both saw makers and accessory manufacturers. Both the single- and dual-line laser guides we installed here are manufactured by Avenger Products (www.avengerproducts.com) and can be ordered from most mail-order woodworking supply catalogs. Be aware that although these products are designed to fit many saws, they may not fit yours. If you order a laser guide and it doesn't fit, return it and try another vendor. With luck, their kit will fit. There are two basic types of add-on laser guides you can install: single-line and dual-line lasers.

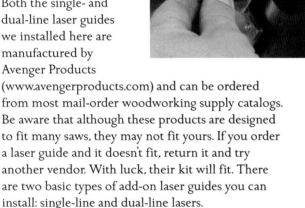

SINGLE-LINE LASERS

The Avenger single-line laser guide kit is simple to install. It comes with extra-long arbor bolts in case your existing bolt isn't long enough. There is also an extra set of batteries. (On some laser guides, these are not installed and you'll have to remove the back of the guide and install batteries.)

Remove the arbor nut

To install a single-line laser guide, start by unplugging your saw. Then loosen the blade-guard screw or bolt and lift up the lower guard to expose the arbor nut or bolt. Next, use the supplied wrench to loosen the arbor nut or bolt (as shown in the far left photo above) and set it aside.

Remove the outer flange

Now you can remove the outer flange that serves as a clamp to hold the blade in place and set it aside, as shown in the bottom left photo.

Install the laser guide

All that's left is to install the laser guide. Simply substitute the laser guide for your outer flange as shown in the bottom right photo. Reinstall the arbor nut or bolt, replace the lower blade-guard linkage, and tighten the screw or bolt. Plug in the saw and power it on to make sure the laser guide turns on. When you turn off the saw, the laser guide will automatically shut itself off.

DUAL-LINE LASERS

The dual-line laser guide kit is similar to the single-line except there are two lasers: an inner and an outer unit. There is also a $^5/_8$" to 1" guide bushing for installing the kit on larger-bore 12"-diameter saws.

Remove the outer flange

To install a dual-line laser guide, start by unplugging your saw. Then loosen the blade guard screw or bolt and lift up the lower guard to expose the arbor nut or bolt. Next, use the supplied wrench to loosen the arbor nut or bolt and set it aside. Now you can remove the outer flange that serves as a clamp to hold the blade in place and set it aside as shown in the middle photo.

Remove the blade

Next, you'll need to remove the blade, as shown in the bottom left photo, to access the inner flange. Slide the blade off and set it aside.

Remove the inner flange

Now you'll have access to the inner flange. Pull this out and set it aside, as shown in the bottom right photo. Take the time now to thoroughly clean the arbor shaft with an old toothbrush. It's also a good idea to store the old inner and outer flange in a plastic bag and label them in case you need them in the future—don't throw them away.

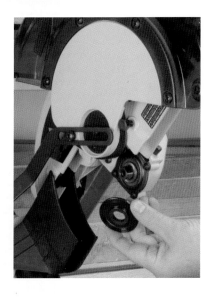

Install the inner laser
Place the inner laser guide onto the arbor shaft, taking care to orient it so that the hex screws and label are facing toward the motor, as shown in the top photo. Check the installation instructions for your specific guide to make sure you orient them correctly. Failure to do so will result in a pair of lines that are way too wide to represent the blade cut line on your workpiece.

Reinstall the blade
Now slide the blade back onto the arbor shaft, making sure the teeth are oriented in the right direction—the teeth should be pointing toward the rear of the saw at the bottom of the blade, as shown in the middle photo.

Install the outer laser
All that's left is to install the outer laser guide. Simply substitute the laser guide for your outer flange, as shown in the bottom photo. Reinstall the arbor nut or bolt, replace the lower blade-guard linkage, and tighten the screw or bolt. Plug in the saw and power it on to make sure that the laser guide turns on. When you turn off the saw, the laser lines will automatically turn off.

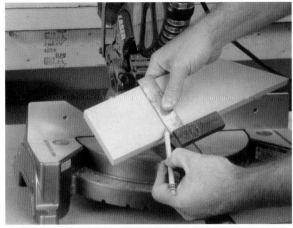

Checking Laser Guides

It's a good idea to check your laser guide alignment periodically to make sure it's still aligned with one or both edges of your saw blade. Some laser systems are adjustable; others are not. Most of the add-on systems are not adjustable.

Strike a reference line

To check a laser guide, begin with a 4"- to 6"-wide piece of scrap wood that has parallel faces and on which the back edge is square to both faces. Then use a try square or combination square and a pencil to strike a reference line across the width of the scrap, as shown in the top photo.

Activate the laser

Before you place the scrap piece on the saw, make sure that the table is clean, particularly where the fence meets the table. Any sawdust or chips caught between the fence and scrap will angle the scrap, resulting in an inaccurate check. Butt the square edge of the workpiece up against the fence as shown in the inset photo. Then slide the scrap over until the reference line aligns with the laser line, as shown in the middle photo. Clamp the scrap in place with a hold-down.

Check the alignment

Now turn on the saw and lower the carriage to make a cut as shown in the bottom photo. Turn off power and examine the scrap piece to make sure the blade cut exactly at the reference/laser line. If it didn't, check to see whether your laser guide is adjustable (for more on adjusting laser guides, see pages 151–152).

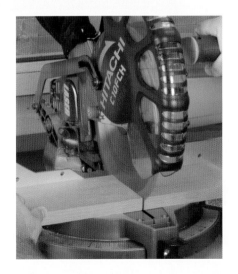

Adjusting Laser Guides

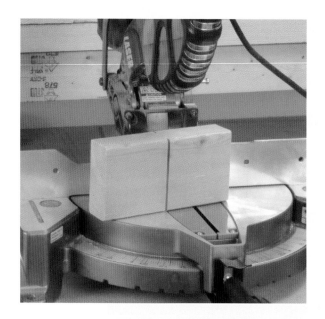

Whether or not you can adjust your saw's laser will depend on whether it was factory-installed or not. Most of the add-on laser guides are not adjustable. And not all of the factory-installed laser guides are, either—consult your owner's manual to see whether your laser guide is adjustable or not. The following adjustment sequence is for a Hitachi saw with a factory-installed laser guide.

Cut kerf in 2×4

To adjust a single-line laser guide, start with a scrap of 2×4 with both faces parallel and the back edge square to both faces. Then cut a $3/16$"-deep kerf in the 2×4 as shown in the top photo.

Clamp the kerfed block in place

Next, align the kerfed 2×4 with your saw blade by lowering the blade until is fits into the kerf in the block. Then clamp the kerfed 2×4 to the fence, as shown in the middle photo, so that it can't move during the adjustment procedure.

Laser warning

Before you activate the laser, take the time to review the laser warnings that came with the laser guide. Check your owner's manual, and look for warning stickers posted near the laser like the one shown in the bottom photo. Remember, just because the laser in a miter saw laser guide is small doesn't mean it can't be harmful. Laser radiation can hurt you. Make sure never to stare directly into the beam, as it can—and will—damage your eyes.

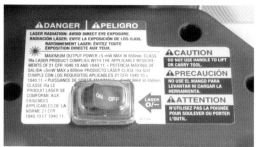

Activate the laser

With the kerfed reference block clamped in place, go ahead and activate the laser. One nice thing about the Hitachi saw shown in the top photo is that the laser can be activated without turning on the saw. This is the opposite of the centrifugal force activated lasers commonly used for most add-on guides. With these you have to turn on the saw to spin the blade before the laser line will activate. What's nice about the separate power switch is twofold. First, there's no spinning blade to worry about. And second, no rotating blade means no vibration—so it's easier to more accurately align the laser.

Align the line with the desired kerf edge

Once you've turned on the laser, you can see how closely it's aligned to one edge of your kerf. On most laser systems like this you can adjust the laser line to align with the left edge (as shown in the middle photo) or right edge of the kerf (as shown in the bottom photo).

Check your owner's manual for the recommended alignment procedure. For the Hitachi saw shown here, an Allen wrench is inserted into a hole in the side of the motor casing, as shown in the top photo. Rotating the wrench will cause the head of the laser

to move to the left or the right. Simply rotate it until it rests directly on either the left or the right edge of the kerf. Then remove the reference block, draw a line across its width with a try square, and make a cut to check for accuracy; readjust as necessary.

▮ TROUBLESHOOTING

As there are many parts and adjustments on a miter saw, there is plenty of room for error—and problems. The next four pages are devoted to common problems and their solutions, including: burning, splintering, and inaccurate 90-degree and angle cuts.

BURNING

Although burning is a problem more common on table saws, you can experience it when cutting on a miter saw for a variety of reasons. If you notice the edges of your cuts are burned or scorched, try one or more of the solutions described below.

Saw blade is dull or dirty

The most common reason for burning during a crosscut is that the blade is dull or dirty. Stop the saw and unplug it. Then raise the lower blade guard and slowly rotate the blade while inspecting the teeth. If you can see a reflection on any of the edges of the teeth, the blade is dull and needs sharpening. Touch-ups can be done by hand with a small file as shown in the top photo and described on page 134. If the bulk of the teeth are dull, have the blade sharpened professionally. If you notice a buildup of pitch and gum, remove the blade and clean it as described on page 133.

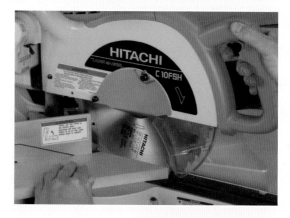

Too slow a feed rate

If your blade is clean and sharp, the next most likely culprit is your feed rate—it's too slow. A slow feed rate leaves the blade in one place too long. The resulting friction of the blade rubbing against the edge of the workpiece can create enough heat to burn the wood. The solution is simple—feed the blade faster through the cut, whether the saw is a sliding compound saw (as shown in the middle photo) or a standard compound saw.

Saw arbor may be bent

Finally, if your saw gets tossed around a lot—like in and out of the back end of a track—the arbor shaft of the saw may have bent over time. To check this, unplug the saw and remove the blade. Then place a dial indicator on the table with the indicator probe up against the arbor shaft, as shown in the bottom photo. Carefully rotate the arbor shaft by hand. Movement in excess of 0.005 inch points out excessive runout, indicating a bent shaft, and it should be replaced.

SPLINTERING

Splintering—where the edge or edges of a workpiece splinter or chip-out during a cut—is a common problem associated with many miter saws. Fortunately, this can be prevented with one or more of the solutions described below.

Saw blade is dull or dirty

Just as with burned edges, the first thing you should look at if you encounter splintering is the blade. Check it to see whether it's dirty or dull. Stop the saw and unplug it. Then raise the lower blade guard and slowly rotate the blade while inspecting the teeth. If you notice a buildup of pitch and gum, remove the blade and clean it as shown in the top photo and described on page 133. Also, if you can see a reflection on any of the edges of the teeth, the blade is dull and needs sharpening. Touch-ups can be done by hand, as described on page 134. If the bulk of the teeth are dull, have the blade sharpened professionally.

Using the wrong blade

Even a blade that's sharp and clean can't prevent splintering if it's the wrong type of blade (lower photo above). Make sure your saw is fitted with a crosscut blade—the more teeth the better. We recommend using a 60-tooth blade on a 10" miter saw and an 80-tooth blade on a 12" saw.

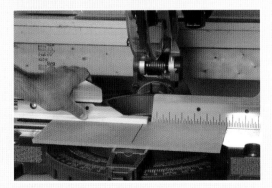

Kerf inserts are too wide

If you're using the correct blade and it's clean and sharp, the splintering may be caused by your kerf plate or kerf inserts. If either of these do not fully support the underside of the workpiece, the blade will splinter the unsupported wood fibers as it exits the bottom of the workpiece. The solution is to adjust your kerf inserts (as shown in the middle photo) or replace a defective kerf plate as described on page 138.

Use a zero-clearance table

Finally, consider using a zero-clearance table. A zero-clearance table is just a piece of ¼" hardboard that's cut to match your existing table. Fasten it to the fixed table portion (not the pivoting table section) with double-sided tape. Then make a cut at the desired angle as shown in the bottom photo. The zero-clearance table will "hug" the blade and fully support the underside of the workpiece.

INACCURATE 90-DEGREE CUTS

A miter saw isn't worth much if it can't make 90-degree cuts with accuracy. Most saw manufacturers provide simple adjustments and easy-to-follow instructions in their owner's manuals for handling the most common causes of inaccurate 90-degree cuts: blade not square to table and blade not perpendicular to the fence, as described below.

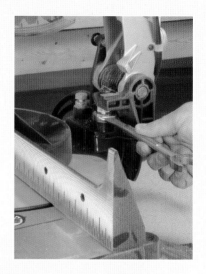

Blade is not square to the table

If your saw blade is not square to the table, the ends of your cut work-pieces will not be square. Start by checking blade alignment. Butt the head of a combination square (or small engineer's square) up against the blade. If there are any gaps between the square head, the blade of the square, and the table, the 90-degree stop needs aligning (photo at right); see page 127 for step-by-step directions for this procedure.

Blade is not perpendicular to the fence

To check fence alignment, butt the head of a combination square (or try square) up against the fence and blade. There should be no gap between the square and the fence or the blade. If there is, you'll need to correct this. Loosen the fence bolts to friction-tight and pivot the fence as needed to eliminate any gaps between the square, fence, and blade as shown in the middle photo. Recheck the alignment and, if it's good, tighten the bolts and check one more time; tightening the bolts can often rack the fence out of alignment. If it's not aligned, repeat this procedure as necessary until it comes into alignment. Then re-tighten the bolts to lock the newly aligned fence in place.

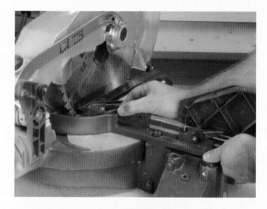

Workpiece may be shifting

Another cause for inaccuracy is that the workpiece may be shifting during the cut. All you have to do to eliminate this possibility is to use a stop (as shown in the bottom photo) or clamp your work-piece in place. Even the best crosscut blade will have a tendency to pull the workpiece slightly as it cuts into the wood, resulting in an inaccurate cut. Use either the built-in hold-down clamps or a shop clamp to securely lock the workpiece against the saw table or fence before making the cut.

INACCURATE ANGLE CUTS

Even if your saw is adjusted properly to make dead-on 90-degree cuts, that doesn't guarantee that it'll make accurate angle and bevel cuts. If you detect inaccuracy with either of these type of cuts, check out the solutions described below.

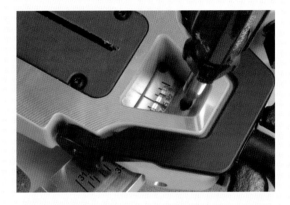

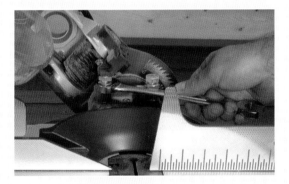

Detents are not aligned

If you find that your miter cuts are not accurate but your 90-degree cuts are, odds are that your detents are dirty or not aligned. The most common detent style is to have notches below the table. Sawdust and chips can build up in these, resulting in inaccurate angles. A brass-bristle brush will quickly remove any buildup with a quick scrubbing. If this doesn't solve the problem, see page 128 for directions on how to check and align detents (top photo).

Stops are not adjusted properly

Inaccurate bevel cuts are commonly caused by improperly adjusted bevel stops. To check the bevel stops, loosen the bevel lock and tilt the blade until it hits the 45-degree stop and tighten the bevel lock. Then butt the angled head of the combination square up against the blade. There should be no gap between the head of the square and the blade. If there is, you'll need to adjust the stop as shown in the middle photo and described on page 129.

Workpiece is creeping

If you check and find that your detents and stops are all properly aligned and you're still encountering sloppy cuts, the problem may be that your workpiece is shifting during the cut. Both a miter cut and a bevel cut tend to pull or push a workpiece during a cut. That's why it's so important to use a hold-down to keep the workpiece locked down solid against the saw table, as shown in the bottom photo.

7 Miter Saw Projects

Although none of the projects featured in this chapter can be made solely with the miter saw, the miter saw plays a big part in the construction of each project. The inherent accuracy of a miter saw is what makes it such a useful tool for these projects as well as many other woodworking and carpentry tasks.

This chapter features six projects: a simple desk frame made from built-up moldings; a frame assembled from crown molding that can hold a mirror, photos, or art; an end table with unique three-way miter joints and decorative inlays; a super-easy-to-make checkerboard that can be enjoyed by kids of all ages; a beveled tray that can be used to store, display, and transport a wide variety of items; and a colorful kids' clothes rack that will inspire even the messiest kid to hang up clothes, hats, and backpacks.

The easy-to-make checkerboard shown here is just one of the many projects featured in this chapter that you can make with the aid of your trusty miter saw.

Simple Desk Frame

Everyone likes to display family photos. But frames—even small ones—can be surprisingly expensive. The simple desk frame shown in the photo at right can be made for about a buck. Besides some scraps of wood, all you'll need to buy is a hinge and some plexiglass or glass to protect your photos. We used a technique called built-up moldings to create the shaped exterior and the intricate interior used to hold the glass, picture, and stand. With this technique you make two simpler strips and glue them together to create a more intricate molding. Each desk frame consists of a frame top and bottom, two sides, and the glass. Grooves in the back of the frame accept the back and hinged stand, as illustrated in the exploded view on the opposite page.

to accept the back with stand. Start by cutting a $^1/_8$"-wide, $^9/_{16}$"-deep groove centered on the thickness of the holder (see the holder detail illustration on page 160). We did this on the table saw with a zero-clearance insert and used a featherboard to press the thin strip against the rip fence for an accurate cut, as shown in the bottom photo.

Rout the coves

To make the desk frame, start by cutting two strips to size—the holder strip is $^3/_8$" thick and $^3/_4$" wide, and the molding strip is $^1/_2$" thick and 1" wide—cut both strips to a length around 24" to 28". (We often make production runs of frame stock like this—you never know when you'll need another frame—and they make nice gifts.) Next, rout a set of three coves in the larger molding strip. We cut all three on the router table with a router fitted with a $^1/_2$" core-box bit, as shown in the middle photo. Each cove is only $^3/_{16}$" deep to create a set of flats on the face of the strip, as illustrated in the frame cross section detail on the bottom of page 160. These flats are approximately $^1/_8$" wide. Use a featherboard and push stick to push the small strip past the bit. This completes the machining on the molding strip.

Cut the groove in the holder

Now you can turn your attention to the smaller back strip—the "holder." This strip is grooved and shaped

Cut the holder to size

To complete the holder, trim off a portion of one of the sides of the U-channel you formed by cutting the groove in the previous step. Here again, we did this on the table saw and used the featherboard to press the workpiece against the rip fence. Note that we positioned the strip so that the waste piece is on the outboard side of the blade where it cannot be trapped (as it could if the waste were cut between the blade and the rip fence). Removing a portion of the U-channel makes it easier to slide the back in and out later when the frame is assembled.

Glue the strips together

Now you can glue the strips together to create a one-piece molding. Apply glue to only the bottom of the holder. Then position it on the molding so the edges are flush, as illustrated in the detail drawing on page 160. When positioned correctly, apply clamps as shown in the middle photo. Spring clamps work great for this, but if you don't have a bunch of these, you can clamp the strips together by stretching and wrapping a scrap of inner tube or other elastic material around the molding. Allow the strips to dry overnight before proceeding. Note that the lip created opposite the flush ends will serve as the rabbet that accepts the glass.

EXPLODED VIEW

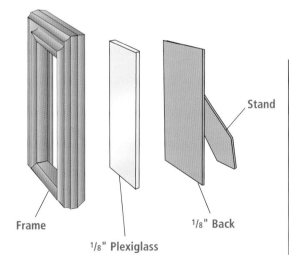

Stand

Frame

1/8" Plexiglass

1/8" Back

MATERIALS LIST

Part	Quantity	Dimensions
Frame top/bottom	2	$1" \times 4\frac{3}{4}" - \frac{7}{8}"$ *
Frame sides	2	$1" \times 6\frac{1}{2}" - \frac{7}{8}"$ *
Plexiglass	1	$3\frac{1}{4}" \times 5" - \frac{1}{8}"$
Back	1	$4\frac{1}{4}" \times 6\frac{1}{4}" - \frac{1}{8}"$
Stand	1	$2\frac{1}{4}" \times 4\frac{3}{4}"$
Hinge	1	$\frac{3}{4}" \times 1"$

* glued up from two strips of wood

Miter-cut the frame pieces

Once the molding strip has dried overnight, scrape off any glue squeeze-out and sand the flush edges smooth if necessary. Miter-cut the frame pieces to the dimensions given in the materials list on page 159. These dimensions will create a frame for most 3×5 photos; alter these as you wish to create a frame of any size. Since these pieces are short, make sure to lock the strip in place with a hold-down before making your cuts as shown in the top left photo.

Trim the bottom frame piece

The back with hinged stand slips into the grooves in the back of the frame. To allow this, the bottom frame piece has to be modified. What you want to do is trim off the holder portion of the molding. We did this on the table saw and again used a featherboard to press the workpiece tight against the rip fence, as shown in the top right photo. Alternatively, when you go to glue the two strips together, you can cut off a short piece of the molding for the bottom and set it aside. This way you won't need to trim the holder off.

FRAME DETAILS

Full-Sized Stand Pattern

4"

1"

1/4"

3/8"

1/2"

3/16"

— Holder

— Molding

FRAME CROSS SECTION

1/8" Hardboard Back

1/8" Plexiglass

Frame

Glue up the frame

With the bottom trimmed, go ahead and glue up the frame pieces. We like to use a band clamp for projects like this, as shown in the top photo. Before you apply glue, it's a good idea to dry clamp the frame and check for gaps at the joints. If you find any, tweak the miter angle as necessary to eliminate the gap. Since these are small pieces, you can easily do this with a sanding block wrapped with sandpaper. When the fit is perfect, apply a generous coat of glue to both ends of each frame piece and apply clamping pressure with a band clamp. Alternatively, if you can find large rubber bands at an office supply store, you can stretch these around the frame. Let the frame glue up overnight. When dry, sand and apply the finish of your choice.

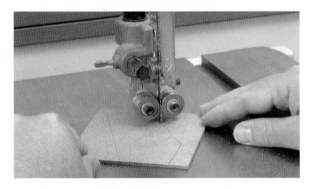

Make the back and stand

With the frame complete, you can make the back and stand. The best way to ensure a snug fit for the back is to measure your frame and cut it to fit inside the grooves. Then cut the stand to rough size and transfer the full-sized pattern shown on page 160 to the hardboard blank. Cut out the stand shape on the band saw (above left photo), or with a saber saw or handsaw.

Glue the stand to the back

The stand attaches to the back via a small brass hinge that is epoxied to both parts. Mix up a small batch of epoxy and apply it to the top inside edge of the stand, as shown in the inset photo. Take care to orient the stand and hinge as shown here. Allow the epoxy to set and then epoxy the other flap of the hinge to the back as shown in the main photo at left. Take care to keep the epoxy away from the hinge knuckle, or it won't be able to move freely.

Assemble the parts

Once the epoxy has cured on the stand and back, cut a piece of $1/8$" plexiglass to fit into the rabbet in the frame (or have a piece of glass cut to this size). Place the glass in the rabbet, insert a photo, and slip the back into the grooves in the frame as shown in the bottom photo. If the fit is too snug, just sand the perimeter edges of the back until the back slips in.

Mirror Frame

We mounted a mirror in this good-looking frame, but you could also use it to display photos or art. Although attractive, the frame shown in the top photo is simple to make, as it's made up of four pieces of crown molding glued together. We sized the frame to accept a standard 12" square mirror tile commonly available at home centers and variety stores. The lengths in the materials list on the opposite page are for the crown molding we used. Since there are numerous shapes and sizes of crown molding available, you'll likely have to experiment a bit if you want your molding to accept a 12" mirror tile. Alternatively, you can simply make the frame and have a piece of mirror or glass cut to fit. The mirror frame consists of four pieces of crown molding, a back, and hanging hardware, as illustrated in the exploded view on the opposite page.

Miter-cut the molding

To build the mirror frame, start by cutting the frame pieces to length from a strip of crown molding. The molding we used has a spring angle of 45 degrees, so we used a crown molding jig to position the molding and then miter-cut the ends at 45 degrees as shown in the middle photo. For more on cutting crown molding, see pages 68–73.

Rout a rabbet for the mirror

The mirror or glass fits into small ⅛"-deep rabbets cut into one of the flats of the crown molding. How wide you can make this rabbet will depend on the crown molding you're using. For optimum support, you want to make this rabbet as wide as possible while still leaving a sturdy lip for the mirror or glass. We routed the flat on the router table using a router fitted with a straight bit, as shown in the bottom photo. If you've got a steady hand, you can rout this by pressing the flat on the molded side of the crown

molding up against the router fence and slide the molding past the bit as shown here. Alternatively, you can cut an angled block and place it under the large flat to hold the molding in position for routing.

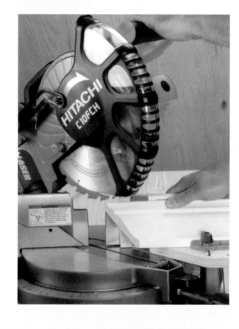

Glue up the frame

The biggest challenge to this project is gluing up the frame pieces. That's because they need to be positioned to create tight miter joints and held in place until the glue dries. Our solution was the clamping jig

shown on page 164. Once you've built the jig, place the frame pieces in the jig without glue to make sure the miter joints are tight. If they're not, sand or file the frame ends until they are, or tweak the miter angle on your saw and re-cut the miter on the frame pieces as needed to get a tight joint. When the fit is perfect, remove the frame pieces and apply a generous coat of glue onto both ends of each frame piece as shown in the top photo. Then insert the frame pieces in the clamping jig and follow the directions on page 164 to use the jig.

EXPLODED VIEW

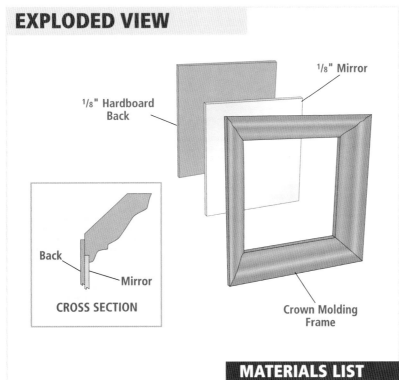

1/8" Hardboard Back

1/8" Mirror

Back

Mirror

CROSS SECTION

Crown Molding Frame

MATERIALS LIST

Part	Quantity	Dimensions
Frame sides	4	$3^1/4" \times 16^3/8"$ crown molding
Mirror	1	$12" \times 12" - 1/8"$
Back	1	$12^1/4" \times 12^1/4" - 1/8"$ hardboard
Screw eyes	2	$1/2"$
Picture wire	1	15" length

Paint the frame

Once the frame has glued up overnight, remove any glue squeeze-out. Now you can paint or stain the frame as desired. Since we used pre-primed molding, all we had to do was spray on a top coat. If your molding isn't primed, apply a coat of primer before spraying or brushing on a top coat. We used a faux stone finish on our frame. Set up a simple spray booth made of cardboard, turn on a fan for ventilation, don a respirator, and spray on a top coat as shown in the top photo. Allow the paint or finish to dry completely before proceeding.

CLAMPING JIG

The mirror frame clamping jig consists of a base and four cleats, as illustrated in the bottom drawing. The cleats position the frame pieces to create tight miter joints. The location of these cleats and the size of the base will depend on the size of your frame and the type and size of the crown molding you're using. To make the jig, start by attaching a cleat to the base with glue and nails or screws. Then position the adjacent frame piece and attach the second cleat—make sure the cleats and frame pieces are 90 degrees to each other. Continue adding the frame pieces and cleats until you've worked your way around the entire perimeter of the frame.

To use the jig, apply glue to the frame pieces and insert them into the clamping jig. Start at one joint and press the mitered pieces together as shown in the bottom left photo. Hold the joint closed for 2 minutes and then stretch a strip of duct tape across the joint to hold it closed. Move on to the next joint and repeat the holding and taping procedure; repeat for the remaining joints. Allow the glue to set up overnight.

CLAMPING JIG ANATOMY

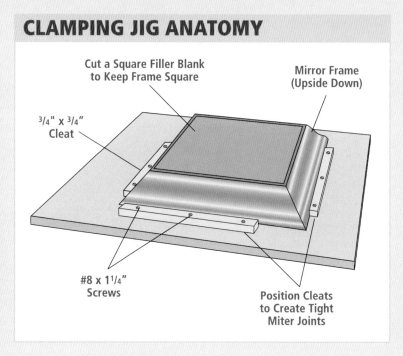

Cut a Square Filler Blank to Keep Frame Square

Mirror Frame (Upside Down)

3/4" x 3/4" Cleat

#8 x 1 1/4" Screws

Position Cleats to Create Tight Miter Joints

Install the mirror

Once the paint or finish has dried, you can add the mirror or glass to the frame. If your frame wasn't made to accept a pre-cut mirror or glass, have a mirror or glass cut to size. Your best bet here is to drop the frame off at a glass shop and have them cut it to fit the frame—we've found that this is more reliable than giving them dimensions and ending up with a mirror or glass that doesn't fit. If you're installing a mirror, it's best to affix the mirror to the frame by running a small bead of silicone caulk around the inside lip of the rabbet in the frame. Then set the mirror in place as shown in the top photo. Silicone caulk is an excellent adhesive, and "gluing" the mirror to the frame will create a stronger unit.

Attach the back

With the mirror or glass in place, you can attach the back. Cut this to fit from $^1/_8$" hardboard. Here again, we used silicone caulk to attach the back to the back of the frame, as shown in the middle photo. The big advantage of using silicone here is that you can remove the back by running a knife between the back and frame back without damaging the frame.

Install the hanging hardware

All that's left is to install the hardware to hang the frame. For this we used a pair of screw eyes set in 1" from the sides of the back and about 1" down from the top edge, as shown in the photo at left. Then we connected the screw eyes with a piece of picture wire, wrapping the ends around the wire next to the screw eyes to create a sturdy hanger, as shown in the bottom inset photo.

End Table

A miter saw, biscuit joiner, and portable router are all it takes to make the attractive end table shown in the top photo. Although we fitted the table with a glass top, you could just as easily insert a plywood top. What's truly unique about the table is that the legs and rails are all joined together with miter joints held in place with biscuits. This creates a three-way miter that's good-looking and strong.

All of the parts are actually made by gluing up strips into an L-shape. This both saves on wood and creates strong parts.

The end table consists of four L-shaped legs joined to pairs of L-shaped front, back, and side rails as illustrated in the exploded view drawing on the opposite page. A glass or plywood top fits into rabbets routed into the top, and rubber bumpers are added to the bottom of each leg to keep the legs from catching on carpet or scratching hard-surface floors.

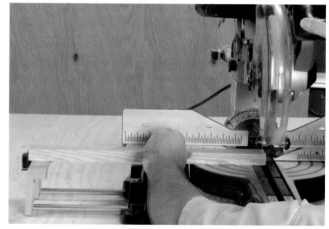

Cut the parts to length

To build the end table, start by cutting the parts to length per the materials list on the opposite page and shown in the middle photo. Since you'll be cutting multiple parts that are the identical length, it's best to set a stop block on the fence to ensure accuracy (for more on using stops, see pages 48–49).

Glue up the legs and rails

With the parts cut to size, begin gluing up pairs of leg sides and leg ends to create the legs as shown in the bottom photo. Make sure the face of each end is flush with the edge of the side. Then glue up sets of side and front/back sides and ends to create the rails. Allow the glue to dry overnight before proceeding.

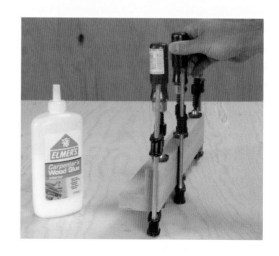

Clean up the surfaces as needed

After the glue has dried on all of the legs and the front, back, and side rails, inspect each part carefully. If you find any glue squeeze-out, clamp the part to the edge of your work surface and scrape off any dried glue with a hand scraper as shown in the top photo.

EXPLODED VIEW

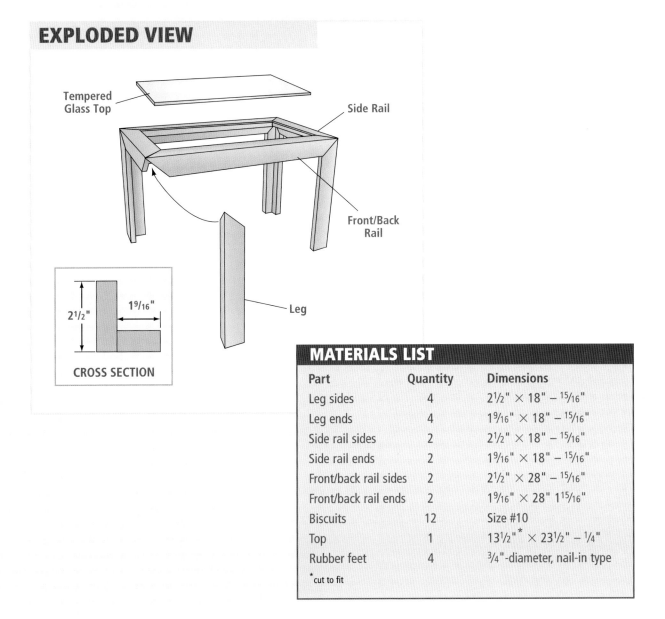

Tempered Glass Top

Side Rail

Front/Back Rail

Leg

$2\frac{1}{2}$" $1\frac{9}{16}$"

CROSS SECTION

Part	Quantity	Dimensions
MATERIALS LIST		
Leg sides	4	$2\frac{1}{2}$" × 18" – $\frac{15}{16}$"
Leg ends	4	$1\frac{9}{16}$" × 18" – $\frac{15}{16}$"
Side rail sides	2	$2\frac{1}{2}$" × 18" – $\frac{15}{16}$"
Side rail ends	2	$1\frac{9}{16}$" × 18" – $\frac{15}{16}$"
Front/back rail sides	2	$2\frac{1}{2}$" × 28" – $\frac{15}{16}$"
Front/back rail ends	2	$1\frac{9}{16}$" × 28" $1\frac{15}{16}$"
Biscuits	12	Size #10
Top	1	$13\frac{1}{2}$"* × $23\frac{1}{2}$" – $\frac{1}{4}$"
Rubber feet	4	$\frac{3}{4}$"-diameter, nail-in type

*cut to fit

Three-way miter joint

As we mentioned earlier, the legs and the front, back, and side rails are joined via a three-way miter as illustrated in the top drawing. Although this may appear to be a complex joint, it's not. Simply put, each part is mitered twice— once on each face. Note: For this joint to fit together tightly, each miter must be accurately cut; so before you make these cuts, check to make sure your miter detents are dead-on at 45 degrees; see page 128 for more on checking and aligning miter detents. If they're not, consider engaging the detent override and adjusting the miter angle with a guide; see page 52.

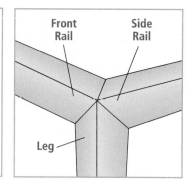

MITERED PARTS DETAIL

Slot for Biscuit

Side Rail

Front/Back Rail

Leg

Front Rail

Side Rail

Leg

3-WAY MITER DETAIL

Cut the first miter

To cut the miter joints, start by angling your saw to 45 degrees. Then work on one set of parts at a time (here we're working on the legs). Set up a stop block to position the leg so the miter cut begins at the top outside corner of the leg, as shown in the middle photo. Adjust your kerf inserts for a tight fit against the blade to prevent splintering (see page 138 for more on this). Then lock the part in place with a hold-down and use a sharp blade to make the first miter cut on each leg as shown in the middle photo.

Cut the adjacent miter

Once you've made the first miter cut on all the legs, leave the stop block in the same place and position a leg on the saw so the mitered face is butted up against the fence as shown in the bottom photo. Then make the second miter cut on each leg. Repeat this double miter cut sequence for both ends of the front, back, and side rails. Make sure to use an angled stop block (see page 53) or a stop block with an extension (like the stop block shown in the bottom photo on page 143) when you go to make the miter cuts on the second end. This is necessary because you'll have just mitered the first end, and a standard stop block won't be wide enough to "catch" the mitered end of the part.

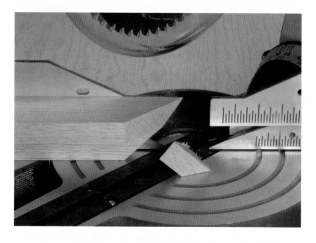

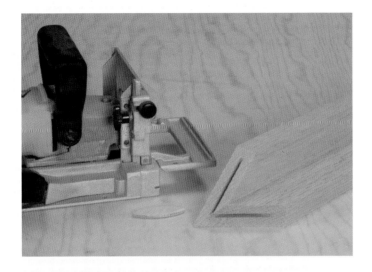

Cut the slots for the biscuits

Once you've double-mitered each of the parts of the end table, the next step is to cut slots in each miter joint to accept the biscuits that will lock the parts together. Begin by setting your biscuit joiner to cut a centered slot on the thickness of the wood you're using (we used #10 biscuits). Each slot should also be centered on the width of the miter as shown in the top photo. Clamp a part to a work surface and cut the first slot. Then rotate the part as needed, re-clamp, and cut the second slot. Repeat this for all of the mitered parts.

Glue up the leg assemblies

With all the slots cut, the parts of the table can be assembled. We used the assembly jig described on page 170 to position and clamp the parts together. The jig is designed to clamp up one pair of mating parts at a time. Refer to pages 170–171 for directions on how to use the assembly jig.

Since the assembly jig can only handle a pair of mating parts at a time, you'll have to glue up the parts over a couple of days, as each joint needs to remain in place in the jig for at least an hour or so to ensure a good bond.

Start by gluing up a leg to a front/back rail as shown in the middle photo. When dry, glue up the opposite end as shown in the bottom photo. Repeat this for the opposite assembly, again gluing a pair of legs to a front/back rail.

ASSEMBLY JIG

Miter joints can be challenging to glue up accurately. Although you can purchase specialty miter clamps for this, you can save the money by making a simple assembly jig like the one shown in the top photo. This jig will position and clamp the pieces together to form a tight miter joint.

Jig construction. The assembly jig consists of a plywood or MDF (medium-density fiberboard) base, two fixed guides, and a clamping wedge, as illustrated in the bottom drawing. (The base on the jig we made is 10" × 24".) To make the jig, cut a pair of 45-degree wedges from scrap wood. Then cut the angled end off each scrap to create the fixed guides (the adjacent 90-degree edges

of the fixed guides are 5" long). As long as your miter saw is cutting accurate angles, this is the easiest way to create a perfect 90-degree corner for the tip of the miter joint. Glue and screw the fixed guides to the base as shown, taking care to create a perfect 90-degree inside corner. Then cut a clamping wedge from a piece of scrap (the long side of the wedge—the hypotenuse, for you math types—is 6½" long). Here again, it's critical that the short adjacent sides form a perfect 90-degree corner.

Apply glue to ends. To use the assembly jig, apply a generous coat of glue to the mitered ends (and slot) of the mating parts, as shown in the middle photo above. Insert a biscuit and press the parts together by hand.

Position clamping block. Place a square of waxed paper in the inside corner of the jig as shown in the middle photo to prevent the table parts from adhering to the jig. Then position the table parts in the jig with the point of the miter joint in the corner formed by the fixed guides. Next, slide the clamping wedge in position as shown in the bottom photo, and apply a clamp across the clamping wedge and fixed guides as shown in the top photo. Apply just enough pressure to close the miter joint, and then wipe off any excess glue with a clean, damp rag.

JIG CONSTRUCTION

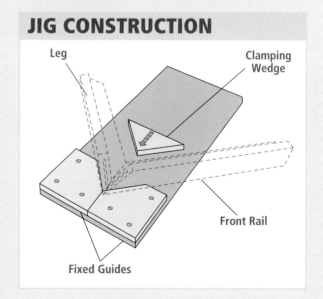

Leg

Clamping Wedge

Front Rail

Fixed Guides

Glue together pairs of legs

Once you've glued up the side assemblies of the end table, you can join the two halves together with the side rails. You won't need the assembly jig for this, as the biscuits will lock the three-way miters in place and they won't be able to slip out of position when clamping pressure is applied. Apply a generous coat of glue to the ends of the mating parts and in the biscuit slots. Insert biscuits and press the side rails into one side assembly; then mate the biscuits in the opposite ends of the side rails with the slots in the remaining side assembly. Apply clamps from side to side, as shown in the top left photo, and adjust the pressure to just close up the miter joints. Allow the glue to set up overnight before proceeding.

Rout the grooves for the inlay

If all your miter joints are tight and you're satisfied with the fit and the look of the table, you can skip the inlay directions and proceed to page 173. If, however, your miter joints aren't as tight as you'd like (even though the biscuits will form a sturdy assembly), or you just want to dress the table up a bit, we offer the following inlay option. Routing grooves and installing inlay to span the joint will both conceal any imperfections and also add visual interest to the table. Because inlay is straight, it's best to use a jig to guide the router to cut the grooves; see below. Once you've built the inlay jig, simply clamp it to any corner of the table, set your router with a $1/4$" bit and a guide bushing to rout a $1/16$"- to $1/8$"-deep groove (depending on the thickness of your inlay), and rout the groove as shown in the center photo.

INLAY-ROUTING JIG

To rout accurate 45-degree grooves for inlay, we designed a jig that uses a router fitted with a guide bushing to create accurate, straight grooves. The jig consists of a $1/4$"-thick slotted top attached to a pair of notched cleats, as illustrated in the drawing. Cut the 5"-long slot to match the width of your guide bushing (ours is $5/8$"), and attach the top to the cleats as shown.

The jig is used by clamping it on a miter joint so the slot is centered on the joint line, as shown in the photo above. Once you've routed the first groove, just reposition the jig to cut each of the remaining grooves at each joint line.

JIG DETAILS

$1/4$" Straight Bit   Guide Bushing

Router Base   Inlay Jig

Workpiece

CROSS SECTION

Glue in the inlay

With all the inlay grooves routed, you can glue in the inlay as shown in the top left photo. Quarter-inch inlay can be purchased, or you can make it yourself. The simplest way to make your own is to rip strips off a ¼"-thick stock, making sure to use a zero-clearance insert in your table saw or band saw to prevent the thin strips from falling into the gap between the insert and blade. It's best to cut the strips a bit "fat" so they'll sit a bit proud of the surface once they've been glued in place; this way, you can sand them flush once the glue has dried; see below. We preferred to work on similar strips of inlay at a time—that is, we attached all the strips in the top of the table first, and then worked on one side of the table at a time. You'll find that you'll need to sand the ends of each strip to a 45-degree point so they'll join together tightly—mimicking the three-way miter joint. Since the inlay is so thin, this is easy to do.

Sand the inlay flush

The most reliable way to end up with inlays that are perfectly flush with the surface they've been set into is to use inlay that's slightly thicker than the depth of the groove and then sand it flush with the surface. The best tool for this job is a random-orbit sander, as it can glide over joints where the grain runs in opposite directions (like the miter and inlay joints here) without scratching the surface, as shown in the top right photo.

INLAY OPTIONS

If you decide to go with the inlay option, you'll need to decide what kind of look you're after: low-contrast or high-contrast, as described below.

Low-contrast. For a low-contrast look, choose an inlay material that is similar in color or a complementary color to the wood used for the table. The example here shows cherry inlay in a red oak table (also shown in the top photo on page 166).

High-contrast. If you're looking to make a statement with your inlay strips, choose an inlay material that's visibly different from the wood used to make the table. The example shown here features a Honduran mahogany inlay set into a red oak table.

Rout the rabbet for the top

With the end table assembled (and inlaid if desired), you can move on to the finishing touches. Start by routing a rabbet along the inside edges of the top frame to accept the top. We used a laminate trimmer fitted with a ³/₈" rabbeting bit adjusted to cut a ¹/₄"-deep rabbet. Run the rabbeting bit around the inside perimeter in a couple of light passes to prevent chip-out, as shown in the top photo. You can either leave the corners rounded (as we did) or square them up. Note that squaring them up with a chisel will save you money on glass, as it can be expensive to create round corners on glass.

Add bumpers to the legs

Once you've routed the rabbet for the top, go ahead and finish-sand all table surfaces and apply the finish of your choice (we applied two coats of satin polyurethane, sanding between coats). When dry, flip the table over and drill pilot holes for the rubber bumpers in the bottom of each leg. Then press a bumper into each hole as shown in the middle photo.

Install the top

Flip the table right side up and install the top. If you're going with a plywood top, cut it to fit exactly in the rabbets and glue it in place; since plywood is dimensionally stable, wood movement won't be a concern here. For a glass top, your best bet is to take the completed table to a glass shop and have them cut a top to fit—actually they should cut it about ¹/₁₆" narrower in both directions to provide some clearance for wood movement. Note that you should use tempered glass here; the glass shop will temper the glass once it's been cut, as you can't cut tempered glass. Before they temper it, have them round over all the edges slightly to prevent cuts. To install the glass, just slip it into the rabbets in the top, as shown in the bottom photo.

Checkerboard

Checkers (or "draughts," as it is known in Great Britain) has ancient roots. The earliest form of checkers was thought to be discovered in an archeological dig; the pieces have been carbon-dated, and it appears that the game was played around 3000 B.C. Strategy books were written about the game as early as the mid 1500s, and in England, mathematician William Payne wrote a treatise on draughts in 1756. The first world checkers championship was awarded in 1847. Over the years, checkers has maintained its popularity. It's still a wonderful way to wile away a few hours in the family room or front porch.

The checkerboard shown in the top photo is easy to build because of the techniques and materials we used There are no concerns about wood movement, which can be challenging to work around with solid-wood checkerboards. The board consists of 64 squares cut from a dimensionally stable engineered wood called MDF, or medium-density fiberboard. This wood product is so stable that you can glue the pieces directly to an underlying base (and to each other) without worry of wood movement. The squares are surrounded by a perimeter edging, and the checkers are cut from 1"-diameter dowel, as illustrated in the exploded view on the opposite page. (Note: Do not attempt this project with solid wood—you'll be sorely disappointed when the wood squares start moving with seasonal changes in humidity and begin popping off the base.)

Cut the squares
To make the checkerboard, start by cutting the 1³/₄" squares to size. The simplest way to do this is to first rip 1³/₄"-wide strips of ³/₄"-thick MDF. Then use the small-piece stop block described on page 176 to cut the squares to length, as shown in the bottom photo. You'll need 64 of these.

Chamfer the squares

The next step is to rout a $1/8$" chamfer on the top edges of each square. This does two things: It provides visual interest, but more importantly, it helps conceal any imperfections or gaps between the individual squares once they're glued together. One way to safely rout this chamfer on the squares is to use a laminate trimmer fitted with a chamfering bit. Place the squares on a router mat as shown in the top photo. The router mat will grip the small piece as you run the chamfer bit around its perimeter—no clamps required.

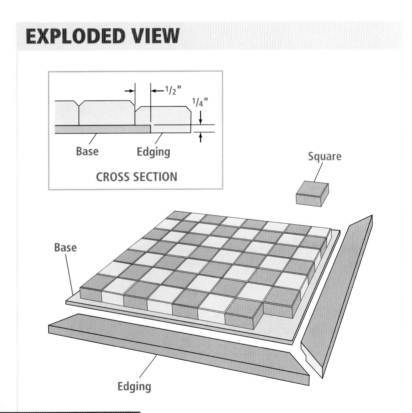

EXPLODED VIEW

Base — Edging
1/2"
1/4"

CROSS SECTION

Square

Base

Edging

MATERIALS LIST

Part	Quantity	Dimensions
Base	1	$15\frac{1}{2}$" $\times$ $15\frac{1}{2}$" $-$ $\frac{1}{4}$" hardboard
Squares	64	$1\frac{3}{4}$" $\times$ $1\frac{3}{4}$" $-$ $\frac{3}{4}$" MDF
Edging	4	$1\frac{3}{4}$" $\times$ 18" $-$ $\frac{3}{4}$" MDF
Checkers	64	1"-diameter, $\frac{7}{16}$"-thick
Felt disks	64	$\frac{3}{4}$"-diameter

SMALL-PIECE STOP BLOCK

You can safely cut small pieces on a miter saw with a small-piece stop block. This simple-to-make jig consists of a clamping base and a flip-up stop connected with a hinge, as illustrated in the top drawing. We used a spare piece of 1¾"-wide MDF left over from cutting the strips to size for the jig parts. The flip-up stop is 3" long, and the clamping base is 8" long. We routed ⅜" round-overs on the end of the flip-up stop so that we could butt our workpiece up against it and still be able to flip it up out of the way (if we'd left the edges square, this wouldn't have been possible).

Attach the stop to the block. To make the small-piece stop block, cut the parts to size, round over the end of the flip-up stop, and attach the hinge. To do this, butt the stop up against the base and position the hinge directly above where they meet. Then drill pilot holes for the hinge screws into each part and drive the screws in to secure the hinge, as shown in the top photo. Since these screws are often brass and can shear off easily, apply some paraffin to the threads before driving them in.

Clamp the stop block in place. The small-piece stop block is used by first positioning it on

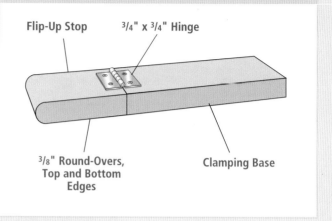

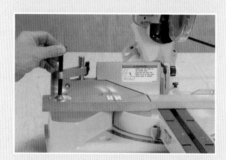

the saw table so that the distance from the rounded end of the stop to the inside edge of the blade is the same as the desired length of your workpiece—for the checkerboard squares, this is 1¾". Once in place, clamp the base to the saw as shown in the middle photo.

Flip up the stop to cut. With the stop clamped in place, butt your workpiece up against the flip-up stop and hold (or clamp) it firmly in place. Then, keeping the workpiece still, flip the stop up and over onto the clamping base as shown in the bottom photo. Now you can safely cut the workpiece to the exact length without fear of trapping it between the blade and the stop. Measure the cut workpiece and, if needed, readjust the clamping base position before cutting the remaining squares to size.

Paint the squares

Once you've cut all the squares to size and routed the chamfers on their top edges, you can paint the squares: 32 red and 32 black. Set up a temporary paint booth constructed out of cardboard, and place a fan nearby for ventilation. Then paint one set of squares black (as shown in the top photo) and the other set red. We found that two light coats provided plenty of coverage (we used a satin-finish enamel spray paint).

Glue the squares onto the base

Let the paint dry at least overnight before gluing the squares onto the base. Cut the base from $1/4$" hardboard—another dimensionally stable engineered wood. Don't use $1/4$" plywood, as it tends to bow and warp with changes in humidity. The squares are glued $1/2$" in from the edge of the base, so scribe a line around the perimeter and use this as a reference. You can apply glue to each piece separately (as shown in the middle photo), but a quicker way is to spread glue onto the base with a small short-nap paint or trim roller. Then all you have to do is apply a small bead of glue onto the mating edges of the squares and press them in place. Once all the squares are in place, you can squeeze them together by placing 14"-long scrap cleats around the perimeter and applying pressure to the cleats with clamps.

Cut rabbet on edging

Set the base and squares aside to dry and begin work on the perimeter edging. These pieces are also $1^3/4$"-wide strips of $3/4$"-thick MDF. Cut these strips long (about 20") so you'll have plenty of room to miter them later to fit around the base. Each edging piece attaches to the base via a rabbet cut into its bottom inside edge. This rabbet fits over the protruding portion of the base that isn't covered by the squares. We cut the $1/4$"-deep, $5/8$"-wide rabbet on the router table with a router fitted with a straight bit, as shown in the bottom photo.

Chamfer the edging

With the rabbet cut in the edging strips, the next step is to chamfer the top edges as you did with the squares. This can also be done with the strips resting on a router mat, or you can cut them on the router table with a router fitted with a chamfering bit, as shown in the top photo.

Miter-cut the edging

After you've cut the rabbets on the edging strips, it's time to miter-cut the edging to fit around the checkerboard. Although we left a $1/2$" perimeter around the base, we intentionally cut the rabbet $5/8$" wide so there'd be plenty of clearance so that we wouldn't need to widen the rabbet or trim the base to get a good fit during assembly. Cut the end of one strip to 45 degrees, and place it on the board so its inside miter aligns with the corner of the corner square. Mark the strip at the opposing corner and cut it to length, as shown in the middle photo. Continue like this, working around the perimeter of the checkerboard until all the edging is cut to fit and the miter joints are tight.

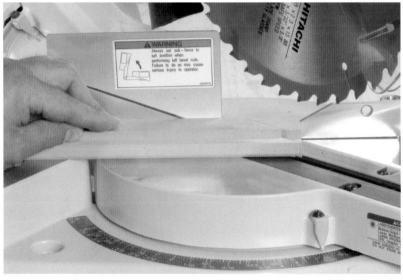

Paint the edging

When you're satisfied with the fit of the edging, go back to your temporary spray booth and paint the edging black (or red, if desired) as shown in the bottom photo. Take care not to paint the mitered ends of the strips, as these need be bare to accept glue during final assembly. Allow the paint to dry at least overnight before proceeding.

Attach the edging to the base

When the paint is dry, go ahead and attach the edging to the perimeter of the checkerboard. Apply a generous coat of glue to the rabbet, and then place the edging onto the board as shown in the top photo. Hold the edging in place with spring clamps and work your way around the perimeter, applying glue to both the rabbets and the mitered ends of the edging, until you've wrapped the board with edging. Set the board aside to dry overnight and start work on the checkers.

Make the checkers

The checkers are cut from a length of 1"-diameter dowel, using the small-piece stop block as shown in the middle photo and described on page 176. Set the stop block up to cut $7/16$"- to $1/2$"-thick checkers, and cut 64 checkers to size (consider cutting 6 additional checkers to length as spares). Then soften the top and bottom edges by sanding or routing a $1/16$" chamfer on each piece. These small parts can be safely routed on a router mat, as shown in the middle inset photo, using the same technique that was used to chamfer the squares.

Finish the checkers

To finish up the checkers, paint 32 of them red and the other 32 black, as shown in the bottom photo (or 35 of each if you made spares). When the paint is completely dry, apply a felt disk to the bottom of each checker (as shown in the bottom inset photo) to prevent them from scratching the checkerboard. Make yourself some popcorn and enjoy a game or two!

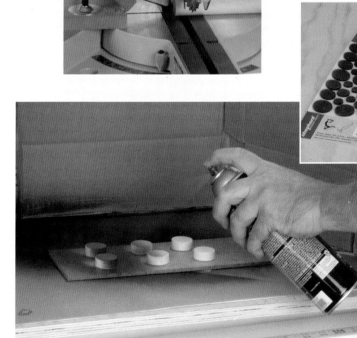

Beveled Tray

A beveled tray like the one shown in the top photo comes in handy for storing, displaying, and/or carrying a variety of items. It makes an attractive display for silverware, can be used to store and organize mail, works great as a basket for fruit, and can even be used to store hardware and tools.

The beveled tray is made up of just six parts: a front and back, two sides, a bottom, and a divider that's locked in place with dowels as illustrated in the exploded view on the opposite page. Although we made ours out of clear Western red cedar, almost any wood will do.

Cut the parts to length

To make the beveled tray, start by cutting the parts to rough width, as shown in the bottom photo. Note that the dimensions given in the materials list on the opposite page are finished dimensions, and it's best to cut each part slightly wider and longer to allow for cutting bevels and miters.

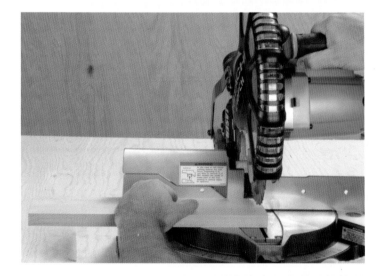

Cut the compound miters

Once all the parts are cut to rough width, you can begin cutting them to their finished size. Start with the front, back, and sides. The ends of each of these are cut at a compound miter. Tilt the blade of your miter saw to 10 degrees and adjust the miter setting to 23 degrees. Then cut each part to its finished width, as shown in the top photo. Make sure to cut opposing angles on the ends of each part.

EXPLODED VIEW

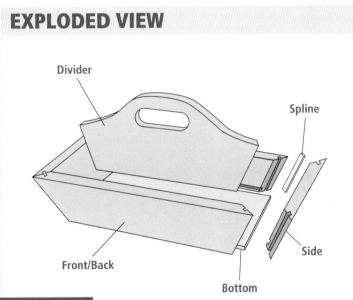

Divider

Spline

Front/Back

Bottom

Side

MATERIALS LIST

Part	Quantity	Dimensions
Front/back	2	$4" \times 14"^{*} - {}^{3}/_{4}"$
Sides	2	$4" \times 9"^{*} - {}^{3}/_{4}"$
Bottom	1	$5{}^{1}/_{4}" \times 10{}^{1}/_{8}"^{*} - {}^{1}/_{4}"$
Splines	4	${}^{1}/_{2}" \times 4"^{*} - {}^{1}/_{8}"$
Divider	1	$5" \times 12{}^{1}/_{4}"^{*} - {}^{3}/_{4}"$
Lock dowels	4	${}^{1}/_{4}"$-diameter, $1{}^{1}/_{2}"$-long

*cut to fit; see text

Bevel-rip the edges

Once you've cut the compound miters on the ends of the front, back, and sides, continue working on them by bevel-ripping the top and bottom edges to 23 degrees. We did this on the table saw, as shown in the top photo, taking care to trim each part to its finished width ($3^5/8$", measuring across the face of each part).

Cut the grooves for the bottom

The next step is to cut angled grooves $1/4$" wide and $1/4$" up from the inside edge of each part. Angle the blade on your table saw to 23 degrees and position the rip fence to make the cut as shown in the middle photo. Make a pass on each piece and then slide the fence over to enlarge the groove to a width of $1/4$" and make a second pass on each part.

Cut the grooves for the splines

The front, back, and sides are joined together on their mitered ends with splines. These splines fit in $1/4$"-deep grooves centered on each mitered end. Adjust the saw blade on your table for a $1/4$"-deep cut. Then place a mitered end flat on the table top and adjust the rip fence over so the blade is centered on the width of the miter as shown in the bottom photo. Next, cut a scrap block of wood at 40 degrees; use it to support the workpiece as you pass the end past the blade as shown in the bottom photo. Cut kerfs on each mitered end of each part. (Note: Although it may look like the fingers are too close to the blade here, they're actually 2" up the angled part being cut.)

Make the splines

Now that the front, back, and sides are complete, you can turn your attention to the splines that reinforce the compound miter joints. Since the splines for this tray are cut from solid wood (versus using an engineered product), you'll need to cut the spline so the grain of the spline is perpendicular to the groove's. If the grain runs parallel, the spline will split when any pressure is applied to the joint.

Here's how to make cross-grain splines safely. Start with a thick piece of hardwood (at least 1"-thick). Cut a $1/4$"-deep groove across the width of the scrap. We did this on the table saw with the rip fence adjusted to create a $1/2$"-wide spline, as shown in the top photo. Do this on all four ends of the scrap so you end up with four splines.

Now reset the rip fence to produce a $1/8$"-thick spline; adjust the blade height to a little over $1/2$". Make sure to adjust the rip fence so that the spline is cut on the waste side of the scrap as shown in the middle photo. Do not position the fence so the spline is cut between the blade and the rip fence. If you do it this way, the spline will get trapped between the two once the cut is complete, and odds are the blade will shoot the spline out backwards. Test the fit of the splines to make sure that they slide into the kerfs easily but are not loose.

Assemble the tray

Before you can assemble the tray you'll need to cut a bottom to fit. The most reliable way to do this is to dry-assemble the tray parts (with splines) and measure from groove to groove from front to back and from side to side. Then subtract $1/8$" from each dimension for clearance and cut a bottom to fit. Take the tray parts apart and slide the bottom in. Reassemble and make sure everything fits before applying glue. With the angled sides, you'll find that a band clamp works best to pull the joints together, as shown in the bottom photo. Use a glue with a long open-assembly time here, or the glue might start setting up before all the parts are assembled. Set the assembled tray aside and begin work on the divider.

Lay out the handle

To make the divider, start by transferring the handle pattern illustrated below to the divider blank. The pattern below is half-sized, so enlarge it to create a full-sized pattern. Alternatively, use the dimensions provided to lay out the pattern as shown in the top photo. Note that the handle hole is centered on the divider and is $5/8$" down from the top of the divider. Lay out a sloping top so the ends of the divider end up flush with the sides of the tray.

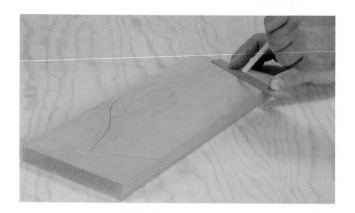

Cut the divider to shape

Once you've laid out the handle pattern on the divider, you can cut it to shape. We cut the top curve with a saber saw (as shown in the middle photo), but you could also use a coping saw. To cut out the handle hole, it's easiest to drill a pair of 1"-diameter holes, $2^1/_2$" from center to center, first and then remove the waste between the holes with a saber saw or coping saw.

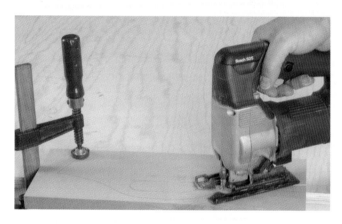

DIVIDER PATTERN

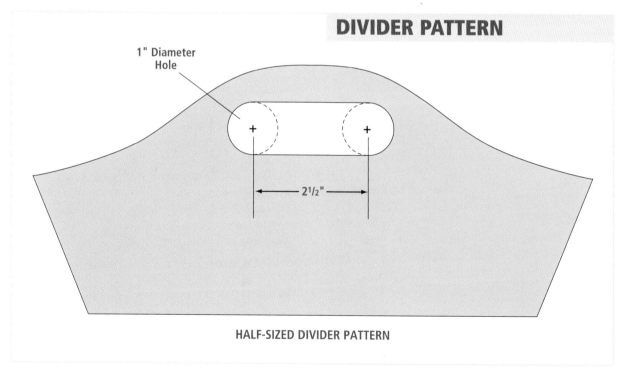

1" Diameter Hole

$2^1/_2$"

HALF-SIZED DIVIDER PATTERN

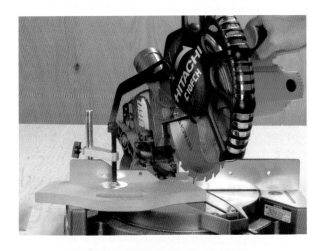

Miter the divider ends

To complete the divider, miter-cut the ends at 23 degrees to fit inside the tray, as shown in the top photo. The most accurate way to do this is to cut the divider a bit wide and slowly sneak up on the final width, taking a series of light cuts and checking the fit along the way.

Install the divider

When the divider fits snug in the tray, all that's left to do is to secure it to the tray. We used two wooden "nails"—$1/4$" dowels—to secure each end. Start by cutting the four dowels to a length of $1^1/2$". Then center the divider from front to back in the tray and hold it in place with one hand while drilling two holes through the sides and into the divider as shown in the middle photo. Drill each hole about $1^1/4$" deep.

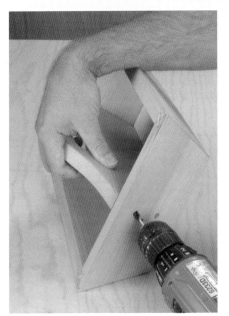

Then apply a dollop of glue inside each hole and tap the lock dowels in place as shown in the bottom photo. Repeat this procedure for the opposite end of the divider. The dowels should sit proud a bit from the sides, so use a fine-tooth saw or chisel to cut them flush with the sides. Sand them smooth along with the rest of the tray and apply the finish of your choice (we applied two coats of satin polyurethane, sanding between coats).

Kids' Clothes Rack

What better way to get youngsters to keep clothes and other goodies off the floor than a colorful rack like the one shown in the top photo. Cheerful primary colors say "this kid-sized rack is just for you." What's more, this pint-sized clothes rack is easy to build. It consists of a post held upright by four feet. Six pegs made from lengths of ³/₄" dowel offer two levels of organization. The upper pegs can be used by taller kids and the lower pegs by smaller siblings. Or, the lower pegs are convenient for hanging backpacks and other kid stuff. Or... the rack can grow with the child—young kids use the lower pegs and graduate to the higher pegs as they age. Any way you use it, this colorful rack will be a welcome addition in almost any kid's room.

Miter the post end

To make the kids' clothes rack, start by cutting the parts to size per the materials list on the opposite page. Although it's not absolutely necessary, we miter-cut the end of the post for appearance. Set the miter angle on the saw for 45 degrees and miter the end of the post. Rotate the post 90 degrees and miter again; repeat for the two remaining uncut sides. You should end up with a pointed post as shown in the middle photo.

Lay out the peg locations

Next, lay out the peg locations on the post. To prevent the holes from intersecting and weakening the post, lay out the top set of peg holes starting 10" down from the top of the post and then stepping down to 11", 12", and 13" as you work around the post as shown in the bottom photo. The two lower peg hole locations are 20" up from the bottom of the post. Each hole is centered on the thickness (or width) of the post.

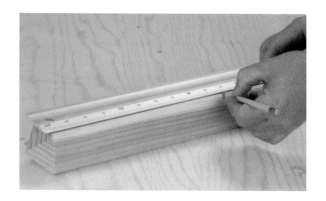

Drill the holes for the pegs

With the holes located, use the angled drilling jig described on page 188 along with a $^3/_4$"-diameter drill bit to drill the holes at each peg location, as shown in the top photo. Clamp the jig at each location so the hole in the jig is centered on the mark that you made to locate the hole.

MATERIALS LIST

Part	Quantity	Dimensions
Post	1	2" × 42" – 2"
Feet	4	$5^1/_2$" × 12"* – $^3/_4$"
Pegs	6	$^3/_4$"-diameter, $4^1/_2$"-long

*rough size of blank; see text

EXPLODED VIEW

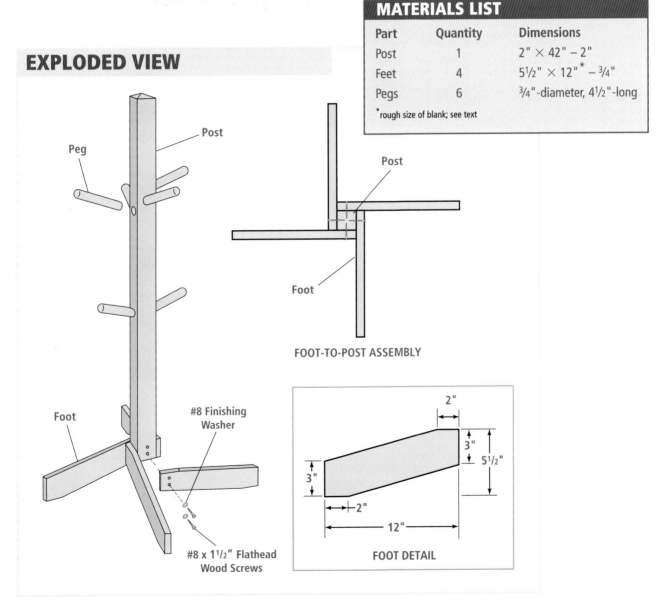

Peg

Post

Foot

#8 Finishing Washer

#8 x $1^1/_2$" Flathead Wood Screws

Post

Foot

FOOT-TO-POST ASSEMBLY

FOOT DETAIL

Cut the feet to size

With the post complete, you can start work on the four feet that support the post. Each foot is cut from an oversized blank. We used the wide-angle jig (with the miter angle set to 30 degrees) described on pages 116–119 to cut the angles on the top and bottom of each foot, as shown in the top photo. See the foot detail illustration on page 187 to locate the start and stop points of these angled cuts.

ANGLED DRILLING JIG

Drilling angled holes is easy with this simple shop-made angled drilling jig. The jig is made up of two parts: an angled block and a clamping cleat. We made the angled block from a scrap of leftover post. The clamping cleat is a 3" × 4" scrap of ¾" stock.

Drill the peg hole. To make the angled drilling jig, start by drilling a ¾"-diameter hole perpendicular to the face of the block, as shown in the photo at left.

Cut the block at an angle. Next cut the block at the desired peg angle (in our case, 25 degrees), as shown in the photo at right. Next, cut the block to length (3"). The beauty of this technique is that the accuracy of the hole angle is provided by the miter saw—and not by the drill.

Assemble the jig.
Attach the clamping cleat to the angled block with glue and clamps as shown in the bottom photo. The angled drilling jig is now ready to use. Just clamp it in place and drill the hole—the angled block will guide your bit into the workpiece at the correct angle.

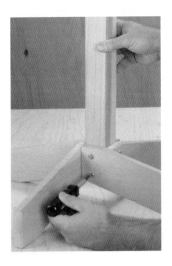

Attach the feet to the post

Once you've drilled the peg holes and made the feet, you can attach the feet to the bottom of the post with screws, as shown in the top photo. We used countersinking washers for appearance, but you could just screw the feet in place.

Add the pegs

Finally, cut the pegs to length, round over the ends as described in the sidebar below, and glue them into the peg holes. Before we did this, however, we dismantled the clothes rack, sanded all the parts, and painted the parts with bright primary colors. If you paint the parts, make sure to wrap masking tape around the ends of the dowels to keep them free of paint so the glue will create a strong bond when they're inserted in the post holes.

ROUNDING OVER DOWEL ENDS

You can quickly round over the ends of your pegs on a router table, using a router fitted with a ³⁄₈" round-over bit. Here's how.

Set up the auxiliary fence. Insert the round-over bit and raise the bit to cut a full ³⁄₈" profile. Then adjust the router table fence so the face of the fence is flush with the bearing on the round-over bit. To rout the round-over, you need to present the dowel to the bit so the dowel is perfectly centered on the bit and rubs up against the bearing. This would be almost impossible to do freehand. That's why we clamp an auxiliary fence to the tabletop (see the bottom left photo). Position the auxiliary fence so the center of the dowel and the bit are aligned.

Basic technique. Now you have a way to accurately and safely guide the dowel against the bit. Turn the router on and, with the dowel pressed up against the auxiliary fence, push the end of the dowel into the spinning bit. As soon as it bottoms out against the bearing, start rotating the dowel counterclockwise until the entire end is rounded over, as shown in the photo above.

METRIC EQUIVALENCY CHART

Inches to millimeters and centimeters

inches	mm	cm	inches	cm	inches	cm
1/8	3	0.3	9	22.9	30	76.2
1/4	6	0.6	10	25.4	31	78.7
3/8	10	1.0	11	27.9	32	81.3
1/2	13	1.3	12	30.5	33	83.8
5/8	16	1.6	13	33.0	34	86.4
3/4	19	1.9	14	35.6	35	88.9
7/8	22	2.2	15	38.1	36	91.4
1	25	2.5	16	40.6	37	94.0
1 1/4	32	3.2	17	43.2	38	96.5
1 1/2	38	3.8	18	45.7	39	99.1
1 3/4	44	4.4	19	48.3	40	101.6
2	51	5.1	20	50.8	41	104.1
2 1/2	64	6.4	21	53.3	42	106.7
3	76	7.6	22	55.9	43	109.2
3 1/2	89	8.9	23	58.4	44	111.8
4	102	10.2	24	61.0	45	114.3
4 1/2	114	11.4	25	63.5	46	116.8
5	127	12.7	26	66.0	47	119.4
6	152	15.2	27	68.6	48	121.9
7	178	17.8	28	71.1	49	124.5
8	203	20.3	29	73.7	50	127.0

mm = millimeters   cm = centimeters

Miter Saw Fundamentals Photo Credits

Photo courtesy of Bench Dog, Inc. (www.benchdog.com): page 35 (middle top photo).

Photos courtesy of Bosch Power Tools (www.boschtools.com): page 9, page 10, page 11, page 25 (both), page 27, page 32 (bottom), page 34 (bottom right), page 36 (middle and bottom), page 77 (top right and bottom).

Photos courtesy of Delta Woodworking Tools (deltawoodworking.com): page 32 (middle left), page 33 (middle), page 34 (bottom middle).

Photo courtesy DeWalt Tools (www.dewalt.com): page 26.

Photos courtesy of Freud, Inc. (www.freudtools.com): page 30 (middle), page 31, page 82 (top), page 83 (top).
Photo courtesy of Hitachi Tools (www.hitachi-koki.com/powertools): page 8.

Photos courtesy of Makita USA (www.makita.com): page 24, page 34 (bottom left).

Photos courtesy of Woodhaven (www.woodhaven.com): page 33 (top), page 35 (middle bottom), page 36 (top photos).